ANN — Be glad
this boy took
you for the Ducks!!
✗ The Babe

the BABE in BOYLAND

by

THE FABULOUS SPORTS BABE

with Neal Karlen

ReganBooks

An Imprint of HarperCollinsPublishers

HarperCollins books may be purchased for educational, business, or sales promotional use. For information please write: Special Markets Department, HarperCollins Publishers, Inc., 10 East 53rd Street, New York, NY 10022.

FIRST EDITION

Designed by Joseph Rutt and Liane Fuji

Library of Congress Cataloging-in-Publication Data
Donnellan, Nanci.
   The babe in Boyland / The Fabulous Sports Babe with Neal Karlen. — 1st ed.
      p.   cm.
   ISBN 0-06-039188-X
   1. Sports—United States. 2. Donnellan, Nanci—Views on sports. 3. Sportscasters—United States—Attitudes.   I. Karlen, Neal. II. Title.
GV706.8.D66   1996
796'.0973—dc20   96-38198

96 97 98 99 00 ❖/RRD 10 9 8 7 6 5 4 3 2

To all the friends who have helped me get here . . .
and especially those who didn't

Acknowledgments

Thanks . . . that's what this is all about . . . right¿¿¿

Phil and Jenette . . . for believing so long ago . . . Joe Fasi . . . the original Babe believer . . . ABC . . . Bob Callahan . . . and Shelby Whitfield . . . for taking the stand early on on what could be accomplished . . . Jane Steinberg . . . and Lynn Andrews . . . for still believing . . . David Kantor and Marty Raab . . .

Jim Cutler . . . the icing on the Babe show . . .

Wilma . . . Janet Magelby . . . I cherish as my friend—and she sees me only as her "marketing rag" . . .

The brilliant Bill Cronin . . .

Dargie Golf in Memphis . . . because it's my book and they make my clubs . . .

Jeff Smulyan and Stuart Layne . . . who are true friends . . . and who introduced me to Lisa . . .

Lisa Miller . . . my friend . . . sounding board . . . who changed my life forever.

Me with my Hooterville buds, Bob and Kathleen Byrne. Bob ran reconnaissance for the "escape"...

Jennifer Rudolph Walsh at the Virginia Barber Agency . . . thank you for being good . . .

Judith Regan and Kristin Kiser at ReganBooks . . . thanks for putting this book together . . . and thank you to everyone else at HarperCollins who helped out . . .

Dan and Jo Johnson whose support has never wavered . . .

Roger Allen . . . who gave me my first job in radio . . .

Peter Kline . . . who makes me happy on a daily basis . . .

Tommy Connolly. . . . who has been there for me throughout the entire ride . . .

Tillie . . . who I wish could learn to drive . . .

The Lamb family . . .

My cousin Ernestine . . . who threatened me if I didn't put her in here . . .

Steve Bornstein and Howard Katz at ESPN.

Contents

The Good, the Bad, and the Gillooly

[written on Babe's ESPN stationery]

To: My Legions, my fans, Babe-aholics everywhere

From: The Fabulous Sports Babe

Re: Getting a life (yours) and writing a life (mine)

Not long ago, publisher and idol-maker Judith Regan came uninvited over to my stately home on the outskirts of **Hooterville, U.S.A.** Opportunity was knocking, but having no idea who this interloper was I sensed trouble.

As is known by my loyal radio listeners—or at least those of my admirers whose memory banks haven't been melted shut by a lifetime of consuming pizza and aerosol cheese—I am a member of the Federal Witness Protection Program. The Fabulous Sports Babe, as it were, has no need for new friends.

Annoyed, I watched through a peephole as this Judith Regan tap-danced around the dented satellite dish in my front yard, then walked a wide veer around the rusting hulk of my beloved Dodge Dart that sits dying on the lawn. Hoping to impede the trespasser's progress, I unleashed a series of sound effects I usually save for the radio when hanging up on callers who've fouled my show's waters.

Fingering my keyboard of appropriate noise, I began with a Beavis and Butt-Head nitwit giggle, followed with a bomb blast that would have won a war. I then sent out the feared Gillooly—the sound of iron pipe hitting human knee, a crunch meant to evoke memories of Tonya Harding's industrious ex-husband. With a final sound effect—HOO-WAH!—I expected to see this intruder hightail it.

But this woman Judith walked on, unaware or unafraid of the Babe's might or the force of my wrath. She strolled right up to my

Airstream trailer and banged on the door. *What up wit' dat?*

I was not impressed by her single-mindedness, nor by the fact that she'd somehow found out where the Fabulous Sports Babe lives. Intruders and degenerate Babe-aholics often find their way, and their skeletons are usually found in March when the snow melts.

I asked Sportsboy for his opinion. Sportsboy, my all-purpose lieutenant on "The Fabulous Sports Babe Show," as well as my personal slave, asked that I first unchain him from the radiator.

"No way," I told Sportsboy. "You haven't even finished your chores." I reminded him that I could easily find another Sportsboy willing to screen my calls, scrub my bathroom, and jump at the every whim of the Fabulous Sports Babe.

Sportsboy whimpered. Then, straining against his manacles, he looked out the window and guessed that the fashionably dressed woman pounding on the Airstream was a panicked widow of a *Fantasy* Football or *Rotisserie* Baseball league **moron.** Having probably lost a spouse to this idiotic exercise in jerking off to sports statistics, the poor soul probably just wanted some advice.

"Let her in!" Sportsboy whimpered, hoping he'd be rescued.

"Oh, all right," I said. "After all, I'm a Good Samaritan, and there is nothing I loathe more than ***Fantasy sports league geeks,*** or pity more than their mates." If these nitwit fantasy players want to waste their time and money knocking themselves out playing their little head games, fine. But please do not bore us all with your ridiculous obsession by calling my radio show. All these fantasy league geeks should be put on a remote island and cut off from the rest of the world. There they could be statistics assholes to their hearts' delight. To me, they are the ultimate examples of people who need to **get a job, get a haircut, GET A LIFE!**

"You *are* a Good Samaritan," Sportsboy said, sucking up, as usual and required, to the boss. And so, jumping into fate, I opened the door of the trailer.

"Fabulous Sports Babe!" Judith Regan began, seeing me for the first time. What up wit' dat? I thought as I scoped out the trespasser.

I looked, as usual, divine. Judith, who I later learned is famous as the unimpressible editor, was impressed. "You are a radio legend, you are part of our iconography, you are a book!" she proclaimed. "Who else could have helped settle the National Hockey League strike or get Roger Clemens to limo chicken to your home in Hooterville from his Rhode Island restaurant? Who else would, in the middle of an interview with National Basketball Association commissioner David Stern, threaten to 'whip his butt' in a game of 'horse'?"

She had a point, whoever this woman was. After providing me with a list of references and her fingerprints, Judith was finally cleared to enter the Airstream. She was who she said she was. Judith then asked me to compose a volume that would appeal to my vast radio and television audience of sports freaks and truth seekers. She wanted to distill the essence of me, the Fabulous Sports Babe. **HOO-WAH!**

Though flattered, I told Judith to ***blow me.*** The Fabulous Sports Babe, I told her, was not for sale. Now that I'd reached the mountaintop of sports radio and television success, I was not about to compose some bogus quickie book to rip off my loyal fans.

However, skewering in print my even more loyal enemies appealed to me greatly. I thought of Greg Norman, that *golf-ing* ***weasel*** *and PR* ***scam-meister,*** and imagined new ways to dissect him in print. I then conjured the image of Donald Fehr, head of the baseball player's union, and drooled. **Don Fehr is the most disgusting sleazebag and despicable human being in the world.** He doesn't care about the game or the fans. He just wants to screw everybody.

The thought of DIVINE BABE RETRIBUTION appealed to me. "Maybe, just maybe, I'd be interested in doing a book," I finally said to Judith Regan. Judith kept at me that day like a jungle predator, relentless in her belief that there was a history-making book bubbling inside me. I could make it a real book, she promised, with all the depth, honesty, and sick humor of classic literature.

Hmm, *Classic Literature,* I thought. You know, it is important to me for people to know that the Fabulous Sports Babe doesn't just go home to her trailer every day after work, grab a fistful of Slim Jims, and put her feet up on the coffee table. No, I don't drive the channel changer for six hours each night, hopping between every sporting event up to and including ice-fishing and shoe hockey.

In truth, it's the tones of *opera*, rather than **professional wrestling,** that visitors hear in the Sports Babe's trailer. And hanging on the walls of my Airstream are genuine prints—art, for God's sake, not those autographed lithographs of Johnny Unitas with a thumb up his ass.

And so I mulled over Judith Regan's proposal. Perhaps, I thought, if I wrote a book that began with some lines from classic literature it would show the world that the Fabulous Sports Babe is far deeper and more cultured than your average idiot sports talk show host. So I began noodling around with a few opening sentences to begin my would-be classic.

I would steal, but from the masters.

Book Opening #1: "Call me Babe—Ishmael is the third string noseguard for the Winnipeg Blue Bombers."

Book Opening #2: "It was the best of times, it was the worst of times. The Fabulous Sports Babe had become the most beloved radio presence since Franklin Roosevelt, but the world of athletics had grown rotten with greedy players, idiot fans, and owners who needed to be told to go directly to hell."

Opening #3: "I saw the best minds of my generation destroyed by madness, starving hysterical

naked, dragging themselves though the negro streets at dawn looking for an angry fix. Wait a minute—were those the best minds of my generation or blue section New York Rangers fans after a game?"

I sent these sample starts to Judith, who told me that all she wanted from me was a volume where I was just myself—the Fabulous Sports Babe, philosopher, queen, empress of the airwaves. I didn't have to quote *Moby Dick, A Tale of Two Cities,* or even *Howl.* **Whew!**

Still, Judith said, it might make my fans more comfortable if I managed to get one of my pet phrases into the book's first paragraph. "Like calling Portland, Oregon, 'the plumber's *butt* of America'?" I asked.

Perfect.

All right, I said, I'll do it—for art's sake.

One
What Becomes
a Legend Most?

ON-AIR

ANNOUNCER: And now, the woman who thought Super Bowl XXX was a film playing at a Times Square movie house . . . the Fabulous Sports Babe!

FABULOUS SPORTS BABE (à la Jack Nicholson in *The Shining*): **HONNEEEE, I'M HOOOOME!** HOP UP HERE DARLINGS NEXT TO MOTHER, NESTLE CLOSE TO THE ORIGINAL MISS FIRECRACKER! TODAY's TOPIC IS LEGENDS, **NAMELY ME.** WHAT BECOMES A LEGEND MOST, OH RICH BOY ON A CAR PHONE BOTHERING **THE BABE FROM PORTLAND,** OREGON, THE **PLUMBER's BUTT OF AMERICA?**

RICH BOY: I'm a virgin, Babe, first-time caller, be gentle!

BABE'S MAGIC KEYBOARD OF SOUNDS: *HOO-WAH!*

FABULOUS SPORTS BABE: OK, NOW HURRY UP AND ANSWER THE QUESTION, GOMER, BECAUSE **WE'RE ONLY ON THIS PLANET FOR A FINITE TIME!**

RICH BOY: First hit me Babe, hit me! Give it to me Mommy, give it to me!

BABESOUNDS: *CLANGGG! CLANGGG!!* (The sound of a hammer hitting metal, followed by . . .) *HEH HEH HEH HEH HEH* (the nitwit gurglings of Beavis and Butt-head).

FABULOUS SPORTS BABE: ARE YOU PREPARED FOR YOUR EXERCISE IN **BABE-OCRACY?** CAN YOU TELL ME WHAT BECOMES A LEGEND MOST?

RICH BOY: I think I heard that Vince Lombardi's heart is frozen in a refrigerator with Walt Disney's brain. Say Babe, can we talk fantasy football? Because I own five teams—

FABULOUS SPORTS BABE (profoundly unhappy): **What're you smoking, Rich Boy?** (The caller is given the *Gillooly*—the sound effect of a pipe cracking a knee is heard across the country's airwaves.) I still feel dirty! Incoming! (The sound of an exploding megaton bomb announces the end of Rich Boy's call, self-respect, and any notion that he is anything less than an utter geek. Failing his exercise in Babe-ocracy, Rich Boy turns off his radio, walks into the ocean abutting Portland, and drowns himself.)

OFF-AIR

With idiots like this calling me every day and cluttering my brainpan with noxious babble, can you begin to see what I, the Fabulous Sports Babe, am up against as I try to find my proper place in the pantheon of radio golden-throats? Was it Walt Whitman or Walter Alston who first said, *"I hear America belching and griping and offering their idiot opinions on Albert Belle's attitude problems"?*

Well let me tell you, sugar babies, those voices are out there, after my hide and your attention. Two hundred thousand **Goobers, Rich Boys,** and **Bubbas** a month call my radio program, and around one thousand of those disembodied voices make it on the air each week. They call me, come to me, mother and babe, for a shoulder to lean on, an ear that will listen, or an ass to take a bite out of.

Well, my ass and my opinions are my own, and may not be reproduced without the express written consent of my own ESPN2, the only cable network to feature twelve hours of daily programming consisting of surgically enhanced spokesmodels in skintight spandex going north and south on pogo sticks. **HOO-WAH!**

That said, I must unfortunately repeat my dilemma: What becomes a legend most? Especially when that legend is *moi,* the Fabulous Sports Babe, **the most justly celebrated radio voice since Paul Harvey?** A woman whose tonsils, like Harvey, made history with a radio microphone by facing down life's horrors—in my case, spending years getting postgame locker room comments from the naked, wet,

**Could I look
any more
divine?**

and wretched refuse known as the Tampa Bay Buccaneers?

What becomes a Fabulous Sports Babe such as this, I've decided, little darlings, is in fact a book, a testament, a document that lasts longer than Charlie Sheen's marriage. When an eminence such as myself reaches the top of the mountain, she has no choice but to begin playing for history.

Why? Because now, sadly, my Babe-a-sultry tones disappear each day into the radio ether, vaporized as fast as professional athletes in a stadium parking lot running away from orphans requesting free autographs. It is for those orphans, and for future generations of scientists, that I now set pen to paper in order to offer the secrets of existence, as well as the answer to how one professional basketball team, the Minnesota Timberwolves, can be so bad, for so long, in so many different ways. **My beloved Kevin McHale,** *please save that team!*

Sorry, I thought I was still on the radio. I thought I still had to

Top Ten Other Questions on the Minnesota Timberwolves Player Questionnaire

10. Have you ever posed for a magazine wearing black hot pants and a dog collar?

9. How many Liberace records do you own?

8. Do you find yourself attracted to . . . Ahmad Rashad?

7. Do you like movies about gladiators?

6. Who would you rather watch: Tom Chambers . . . or Marilyn Chambers?

5. True or False: Wilt Chamberlain owns the NBA scoring title.

4. Have you ever had fantasies about the Phoenix Suns Gorilla?

3. Can you make love while someone spins a pinwheel in your bedroom?

2. Are you now sleeping with or have you ever slept with Madonna?

1. Are you now sleeping with or have you ever slept with Dennis Rodman?

shout, still had to shove my learned opinion down America's throat in between telling off **boring, pinheaded jerks** and running commercials for hair replacement systems. The medium is the message, and in sports talk radio, you always cut to the chase—even when you're the Babe in the middle of a wise and learned rap.

But shouldn't I content myself with radio, a place where I

already know the rules, long ago broke them all, and have now come to prosper? Many of you, no doubt, might think I have enough of a bully pulpit broadcasting four hours a day on the ABC Radio Network to several million Babe-starved souls over two hundred stations. Don't I risk being labeled a media whore, especially when you factor in that extra hour a day I reveal myself to the cameras—I look divine, by the way—on ESPN2, the only network UNAFRAID TO PROGRAM AN HOUR A DAY OF MIDGET THUMB-WRESTLING?

What more do I really need, when in 1996 *Newsweek* has already dubbed me **"the hottest new thing in the airstream?"** (Babe note to *Newsweek* writer Curry Kirkpatrick: Thanks for the plug. Did you enjoy the complimentary box of steaks?)

I'm not sure if *Newsweek,* in mentioning my hallowed place in the airstream, was referring to my radio network or the trailer I am forced to live in for security reasons. In either case, I accept the mantle of hotness.

It is an honor, an obligation, a duty. For I am not only the first woman to have her own nationally syndicated sports radio talk show, I am also the first sportscaster of any gender willing to tell callers to get a life when they utter idiocies on the air.

In this book, unlike on the radio, I won't have the distractions of repressed and demented callers begging to be humiliated by mommy, nimrods from Utah demanding my spiritual recovery, or sponsors requesting that I not ridicule their products. Finally, I can say what I want, the way I want to.

Now, I can finally say *"Blow me!"* when appropriate, which is often. I can say *"Fuck you!"* when needed, which is sometimes. And best of all, I am allowed to shriek **"Bastards!"** at the people I blame whenever anything goes wrong in my world, my show, or my life. It is for graces such as these that we labor, become legends, write down our stories, and pass them down to future scholars. And frankly, I don't care if you like it.

And so we begin. Unfortunately, some of my devoted listeners—those who move their lips when they read—have no doubt by now set down this tome and tuned in to one of the several hundred sports call-in radio shows that pollute our airwaves like so many tons of Limburger. The Babe, always one to share, doesn't begrudge these shows their listeners or their places on the dial. These listeners are also my most illiterate fans, and I'd prefer they go elsewhere.

At its best, my show is THEATER OF THE MIND. These other sports talk shows are, at best, the outhouse in the rear of the theater of the mind—necessary, perhaps, but not fondly remembered. If nothing else, these other shows give jobs to radio hosts stewing in their own testosterone, who don't know anything beyond **eating pizza, jerking off, and playing fantasy football, today's hobby for tomorrow's serial killers.** There is only one piece of advice I can give these hosts and their listeners: **Get a job, get a haircut, get a life!**

For those of you still with this, fasten your seat belts—we're in for a bumpy ride filled with the brutal and ugly people who populate sports in the 1990s. **Bastards!**

"What up wit' dat?" I imagine many of you Pollyannas now asking. The shock, the horror, how can the Babe be so jaded? What's the matter, dear reader, can't face the fact that no team really cares anymore if their players are solid, God-fearing role models? Please be assured that if any football squad was composed of men of good character, they would finish the season no better than 3–13.

Character is just no longer a part of the professional sports equation. Sure, we like the San Antonio Spurs' David Robinson, but his team will never win because he's **too soft.** He's too nice out on the court. Somehow the Houston Rockets' Hakeem Olajuwon—he's Muslim—is able to separate his religion from the intensity that he brings to the court. But far too many players want to bring their religion into their game, and it just doesn't work. Professional athletics is just too big and violent a business to abide missionaries playing for God.

So should we fans gnash our teeth because our heroes aren't heroes anymore? Maybe we should just redefine what we demand from the men and women we worship.

I remember we got a lot of calls on the radio show when it was announced last year that Mickey Mantle was dying. Younger people would call in and say, "Why are you glorifying him? Mickey Mantle was a drunk who basically killed himself."

Babe Flashback

On July 5, 1968, the Philadelphia 76'ers traded Wilt Chamberlain to the Los Angeles Lakers for Darrel Imhoff, Archie Clark, Jerry Chambers, and an undisclosed amount of cash after the Sixers were unable to sign Chamberlain to a contract. From what we understand, Wilt forced the trade because he couldn't "score" anymore in Philadelphia.

I tried to explain to listeners that he was the Mick—that that alone was enough. I don't blame Mickey Mantle for anything. And to those fans who blame him for the wreckage of his life: **Give me a break, he's Mickey Mantle!** The man was dying!

And when he finally died I broke down in tears, because when I was teeny tiny, even though I was a **Boston Red Sox fan,** I rooted for Mickey Mantle. My family lived all over, and we were on the road so much that the only team I ever seemed to see on television was the Yankees. I would go out into the backyard and pretend I was Tony Kubek, Tom Tresh, and, of course, Mickey Mantle.

He was the one. And when you're the one, people will cry when you die.

The one. Never before has sports been more about the individual reigning over the team. For proof, look at what's happened to Bobby Knight at Indiana. Here, of course, is a good, successful, old-time coach who still comes from the school of leadership where it's OK to tell a team "just shut up and do what I tell you."

But now players ask their coaches why they should shut up. Now, instead of punching them, coaches must explain why and hope the players like the explanation. Bobby Knight could never do this sucking up, and that's why Bobby Knight hasn't won a national championship in so long. Dominant players in high school don't go to Indiana anymore, because who wants to play for a DICTATOR in 1996?

There's just not much a coach can do these days, especially in pro sports. Take what happened one night in Tampa when John McKay, then the Bucs' head coach, was having dinner with some of his players at a local restaurant. A young woman came up to McKay, told him she was from California and used to follow his teams at USC, and asked for his autograph.

The coach complied, at which time one of his players stood up, put his arm around the woman, and invited her to a party that night. The woman said, "No thank you, I'm married. I just wanted an autograph."

At this point the player unzips his pants, places his gifts upon the dining table, and announces to the woman, **"WELL, THIS IS WHAT YOU'LL BE MISSING!"** At this point, coach John McKay begins choking on his food and turning purple. They literally had to Heimlich him and pound on his chest to save his life. Who says coaching isn't stressful?

Nor are players particularly bright. I still remember Booker Reese, who the Bucs signed for a $300,000 bonus in the early eighties. After he got his check, Booker went right down to the local Cadillac dealership and bought a car for himself and one for his mother. He then handed the dealer his $300,000 check from the Bucs and asked for change.

Then there was Eric Turner of the Cleveland Browns, whom I once had on my program shortly before a big game with the Steelers. Here is the transcript:

FABULOUS SPORTS BABE: Eric, talk to me about where your team is in terms of getting ready to play Pittsburgh.

ERIC: We're about an hour and a half from Pittsburgh, and we'll take a bus down there. That's a lot of fun—there's a lot of scenery. . . .

Hello???

Yet who do I think I am to pass such bold pronouncements on who is a loser, a bastard, an idiot, a man worth remembering, a coach out of his time? I am, as it were, the Fabulous Sports Babe, one who knows.

In fact, I know too much, which is why I am in this particular pickle, the plot of which my faithful listeners have been able to pick up on. I used to have another name, but ever since I entered the **FEDERAL WITNESS PROTECTION PROGRAM** I have been known only as the Fabulous Sports Babe.

I like it that way. The name "**Babe**" has brought me to the mountaintop. To not call me "**Babe,**" on my show or on the street, is to not recognize what I've done in my career. It is to disrespect my accomplishments, reduce me to something smaller than I deserve. When I am addressed as "**Babe,**" it is not a sexist slur, but a title.

I am Babe and Babe is me. The voice you hear on the radio is not shtick, not a persona I put on and take off at will. I am the hardest working person in radio, but I'm never faking who I am—or what I know.

Which is how I got into this trouble in the first place. I originally had to go into the Witness Protection Program because I simply knew too much about *everything.* I know who the guy was on the **grassy knoll** that day in Dallas in 1963, and how it was that **Joe Namath** was actually able to beat the Baltimore Colts in the 1969 Super Bowl. I know whether *Babe Ruth really called his home run shot in the 1934 World Series,* as well as what happened to both AMELIA EARHART and KC AND THE SUNSHINE BAND.

The truth is dangerous, as am I. Together we shall set you free. Care to enter my Airstream? **HOO-WAH!**

$\mathcal{T}_{wo}$
Don't Hate Me Because I'm Babe-alicious

I have a young playwright friend whose **Babe-aholic** status has advanced to the point that he's legally changed his name to WILLIAM BABESPEARE. For years, he's told me that my life has all the elements of grand fucking theater. Vowing to write me a Broadway-bound play called *Babe-ita,* he began following me around in order to translate my life in the trailer into a three-act hit. An excerpt from this morning's session.

Scene: A typical Saturday morning at the Fabulous Sports Babe's trailer.

The Babe arises at eleven and rummages through her diplomatic pouches for communiqués from Washington, Moscow, and Krakatoa East of Java. She checks faxes from the FBI, Interpol, and the KGB concerning any new crimes that might have been committed overnight by the Nebraska Cornhuskers football team.

Babe then checks her answering machine, which is filled with messages from would-be suitors begging her to share her divinity with them.

BABE: *Hah! (She scoffs toward the machine and its beseeching voices.) Yeah, right, you morons!*

Babe enters the kitchen, where Sportsboy has been busy baking since five and cleaning since eight. Wearing a leash, he is just able to reach the dog dish with his breakfast of sawdust, pebbles, and Gatorade. Babe is in a good mood.

BABE: *Hey, Sportsboy! You missed that corner behind the refrigerator, you ungrateful idiot! What up wit' dat? Don't you know how critical it is that the Fabulous Sports Babe's Airstream trailer at all times look like a backdrop to a fabulous Aaron Spelling production?*

Sportsboy whimpers, begs, pleads for mercy.

BABE: *Do you know how close I am to relieving you of your duties, eighty-sixing you out of this trailer, and sending you down the mountain to resume your previous pathetic life playing rotisserie baseball and dusting your complete bound collection of* Penthouse Forum *columns? Now stop whimpering, Sportsboy, this is called Mother's tough love.*

SPORTSBOY: *Thank you, tough lover, Mother, savior, higher power, God!*

BABE: *Now, if you promise I'll never again find the goddamn cap off the toothpaste tube or an oven uncleansed, I'll let you go visit your family on Thanksgiving. No, not this Thanksgiving, the one after that. Now, don't let the door bang your ass on the way out of the trailer, Sportsboy. I need to be alone. I must write. I must tell my truths.*

Sportsboy nods and whimpers as the Fabulous Sports Babe takes off his leash. She then places a tracking device on Sportsboy's ankle, and cocks her head toward the door.

BABE: *Finally, some privacy! I really am going to have to give some serious thought to taking applications for a new Sportsboy.*

The Fabulous Sports Babe walks to the coffeepot and takes a sip of the astonishing Caribbean hazelnut coffee that Sportsboy grew hydroponically in his water dish, then ground by hand. Babe nods. Sportsboy will live another day.

Babe walks to the trailer alcove, pulls a lawn mower–like cord, and warms up her diesel powered typewriter: a 1964 Shmenge, a Bulgarian model that Babe picked up for a good price at the 1980 Olympics. Though it is hopelessly outdated, Babe is partial to this typewriter: It's the one on which she typed her Pulitzer Prize—winning book of poetry, *Blow Me, You Ignorant Low-Life Pond Scum.*

Babe sits down and plugs in a cassette of the Metropolitan Opera singing *Carmen* in 1947, with Risë Stevens on soprano in the title role. Singing along expertly in the original Italian, she begins plunking on her typewriter with her elbows, thus leaving her hands free to conduct the opera.

—End of Scene One 🎵

Bubba, that's not writing, that's typing. Let me show you how a real poet recalls the past.

Good morning, dear readers. Did you have a nice night? To be honest, I don't really care. On the rare occasions when I actually do think of my vast audience out there, doing whatever it is they do, I am often repulsed. I see them in my mind's eye forlornly kicking cans in the street, wearing $275 Washington Senators jackets, and waiting desperately until my next show.

Still, just because I'm repulsed doesn't mean I don't *like* you, dear listener. In just the same twisted way, I care deeply about **Sportsboy,** even though he so fills me with revulsion that I keep him chained up. Am I too harsh just because the thought of him roaming free in my trailer—going into my closets and fondling my socks—makes me want to **roll on the floor and jabber in tongues?**

A lovely photo of me and my slave and sidekick, Sportsboy.

Yes, I admit I harass Sportsboy, make him my slave, humiliate him in front of the world from this tiny studio in my trailer. And for what, you may ask?

I torture Sportsboy because, as I've explained to him, he's a symbol of male suffering. He is the **Everyman** who is oppressed by a wife, a girlfriend, a mother. I put him on the radio because he represents every male listener. I offer up to them the Sportsboy as an **ICON. HOO-WAH!**

It's a heroic role for Sportsboy, and he enjoys being a symbol of the harassed man. So Sportsboy is loyal to me, and I'm loyal to him. And in this day and age that kind of allegiance is **everything.**

When I think of loyalty in sports, what naturally comes to mind is . . . NOTHING. I can't remember the last time I even thought about the notion of loyalty. It's no longer relevant to big-time, big-money athletics. In fact, loyalty was probably never important: The history of labor relations in professional sports is an absurd and inconsistent tale of greed, duplicity, and the attempt to give the royal shaft to the fans.

So I'm not one of those Neanderthals who say we should go back to the days when owners could run their teams like little plantations, buying and selling their players like bales of cotton. Back then, players often stayed with their teams for years on end, but that was because they had no fucking control over their own lives—they were indentured servants. They couldn't go anywhere else, unless their owners traded them. That was wrong. The players were fucked.

My own notion of team loyalty went down the toilet in 1976 when the **BOSTON RED SOX—MY TEAM, MY BELOVED SOX**—traded the heart of their lineup away one year after the big 1975 pennant-winning team. Faster then you could say "the ghost of Harry Frazee," the Red Sox got rid of Carlton Fisk, Rick Burleson, and Freddy Lynn in one of those idiotic fits of housecleaning so common in baseball.

Those assholes in management, they always gave lip service to the notion of loyalty, but never had any real regard for it beyond propaganda to be used against players who wanted to go somewhere else. Screw 'em.

So God bless Curt Flood, the star outfielder who told baseball to go **Gillooly** itself when he was traded by St. Louis to Philadelphia in 1970. Refusing to report to the Phillies, he instead filed suit against baseball's "reserve" system, which allowed players to be bought and sold like used cars. Curt got his case all the way to the Supreme Court, but he lost. He never got his due, nor

We told you earlier that Shane Standt was released from jail. . . . He's the one who whacked Nancy Kerrigan in the knee. Well, before I leave you for a week for parts unknown, I give you the:

Top Ten New Jobs for Shane Standt Now That He's Out of Prison

10. Baton twirler in the Walt Disney World parade.
9. Knee Surgeon: "Does this hurt?" *(Bang)* "Does this hurt?" *(Bang)*
8. Executive for the Baseball Network.
7. Backup singer for "Tonya and the Pipe-Wielding Thugs."
6. Mo Vaughn's new hitting instructor. *(Bang)*
5. Jack McDowell's new attitude adjuster. *(Bang)*
4. Professional "Whack-A-Mole" player.
3. Official Zamboni driver for *Disney on Ice* . . . starring Nancy Kerrigan.
2. Stunt Gillooly in the new Jeff Stone movie.
1. Sportsboy!

a slice of the dough he earned for others, the unlucky sonuvabitch.

But it's his legal fight against the reserve clause that eventually led to all these idiot players we now see on television raking in these unbelievable salaries. Free agency began with Flood's losing assault, and I bet almost none of those egomaniacal jocks telling kids to stay in school ever heard of Curt Flood.

So in this new unholy world, questions of loyalty to a city by either players or owners seem almost ridiculous. That said, there are some irrefutable facts that make me think that it might even be OK to let team owners shuffle their franchises around the map like they've been doing in ever-increasing numbers over the last few years.

Now, I have no allegiance to the Cleveland-now-Baltimore Browns ownership. In fact, I fucking hate **ART MODELL** and how he hopscotched his way to Baltimore when the goodies to go got too good. I hate what he did in moving his team and breaking the hearts of all Cleveland.

But when I really think about his situation, I realize that Modell just didn't have what he needed in Cleveland. What he needed was more **luxury boxes,** but none could be added to his old stadium. So then he said he needed a new stadium or he was gone. Modell got *nothing* and, true to his word, he split.

On the other hand, I just don't understand how we can put a man on the moon but can't figure out how to add more luxury boxes to preexisting football stadiums. Why does everybody always need a brand-new stadium?

But if there are Baltimores and Orlandos willing to build those luxury box–choked new stadiums to lure a team, who can argue with an owner of a team in a languishing market listening to offers? Maybe the shuffle of teams we're experiencing is just an historic rebalancing, like what happened in 1958 when the New York Giants and Brooklyn Dodgers moved to California and shifted all of baseball into modern times. Maybe the realignments we're now seeing in all the major sports will settle league lineups for the next forty years.

Babe Flashback

On September 15, 1946, the Brooklyn Dodgers beat the Chicago Cubs 2–0 in five innings when the game was called because of gnats bothering the players and umpires. The Dodgers then decided to eliminate "Gnat Day" from their list of fan giveaways.

I mean, let's get real. What about the poor old **Pittsburgh Pirates,** bless their souls? It's too bad that they don't make steel the way they used to in Pittsburgh, **BUT THAT'S THE FACT, JACK.** The city's in trouble and the Pirates are ripe for picking. Why is that bad? The country's population base has shifted from the **Rust Belt** to the west and south, and how can anybody be surprised when a **Phoenix** or a **Nashville** goes after the **Pirates** or your own failing baseball team?

The world has changed, and the sports have to change with it. Look at **Nashville.** Twenty years ago no one gave a whit about country music, but now it's the number one music in the land. Nashville is now home to the largest music business on the planet—and still this major league–ized city doesn't have a baseball team?

Orlando is another city rightly on the make for bigger things. I remember when Orlando was nothing but the town you drove through on the way to Daytona Beach for spring break. Now it's an industry, and I believe that the people who own the Tampa Bay Buccaneers just might move to Orlando overnight. It's just business, boys and girls, and we're going to see a wave of franchise shifts in the coming years like nothing ever seen before.

Of course, more and more cities facing the loss of a beloved team to a fresher suitor have turned to playing the game too. Now, owners don't actually have to move their teams anywhere. All they have to do is *say* they're thinking of moving, and that is usually enough to push city fathers to literally bend over backward to save "their" team.

A good case study could be made of Seattle, where Barry Ackerley, the guy who owns the **Supersonics,** was able to completely bamboozle the politicians for a new basketball arena. Ackerley was able to get the city to build him a $200 million arena that he didn't have to put a dime into. It was an unbelievable sweetheart deal.

It was during this time that I also realized it was nearly time for me to get out of doing radio in Seattle, where **I was the biggest local thang since Jimi Hendrix.** As it happened, my radio station was also owned by Ackerley, and all on-air personnel were told to chip in to the propaganda campaign surrounding the building of the new arena.

Forget it, I said to my management. Instead, I went on the air and said, "This is the richest family on the planet. Why the hell can't they kick in a couple million for *their* stadium? As it stands, that arena is a shrine to one of the richest families in Seattle."

Following that outburst, I was actually sent a memo by station management detailing how I should exactly word statements about how our owner hadn't spent a cent for his new arena. As soon as I read it, I knew I had to get the fuck out of that town. And I did.

Loyalty **in sports?** We might as well ask our military forces to go back to fighting with muskets and catapults. Still, each team and its collective players must exhibit a certain respect for the community that supports them. This, as is obvious from the paper almost every single day, is not so simple a task.

The problem is that many modern players have an unbelievably inflated sense of their own talent and worth in the universe. They think they are bulletproof. Until recently, even the worst of these athletes have been coddled and sucked off since they were five years old. Their crimes were covered up when they messed up, and it's **WRONG, WRONG, WRONG.**

Now, I don't believe that athletes have a responsibility to be role models for children or anybody else. The kind of people who want and expect athletes to be role models for their children are mostly ignorant rednecks who don't have the brains or the balls to take care of their own kids.

Yet while athletes shouldn't be looked at as guides to life, those jocks also have to realize they have a responsibility not to be seen on the eleven o'clock news getting out of a squad car with jackets over their heads. I just can't believe how stupid these assholes are.

Take, for example, the case of **Michael Irvin,** the All-Pro receiver and trash talk emperor of the Dallas Cowboys. **Great pass catcher, even bigger prick.** He never scored a touchdown without cakewalking through the end zone.

If Michael Irvin thought he wasn't getting the ball enough he'd simply demand more passes. And if he was going out on the town, he never left unless he was dressed like Superfly: a gold necklace, diamond bracelet, diamond-studded gold watch, and a diamond stud in his left ear. **HOO-WAH***!*

Anyway, the case against Irvin begins with him apparently partying with two women in the winter of 1996 in a Dallas motel room. Neither of the women were, as it happened, Irvin's wife, herself a former Miami Dolphins cheerleader. Later, the brain surgeons in Irvin's motel room would describe themselves to the cops as "self-employed models."

A h e m. Anyway, the motel manager calls the police because the noise coming out of Irvin's room suggests hookers and drugs. So the cops bust in and find **THREE OUNCES OF MARIJUANA, TWO OUNCES OF COCAINE, DRUG PARAPHERNALIA, AND ASSORTED SEX TOYS.**

Nice story, huh? But what solidified my notion that Mr. Irvin is a **24-karat diamond-studded asshole** was what he said when the police officer came through the door and into his playpen. "Hey," Irvin reportedly said, trying to talk himself out of the bust, "can I tell you who I am?" Fuck you. LET'S SEE YOU CAKEWALK THROUGH THE PRISON SHOWER. Talk about your geek of the decade.

But wait, it gets even worse. A few weeks after Irvin was busted, a Fort Worth television station reported that he'd continued to buy drugs after he was arrested and indicted on felony dope charges. Unfortunately for Michael, May is a sweeps rating period for local TV news, so the station also went to the trouble of getting Irvin's driver and friend to let them put a camera in his car.

Not to be outdone by the Dallas TV station, the Global Babe Network has obtained a copy of Michael Irvin's daily planner. Let's take a look at Tuesday, May 7, 1996. . . .

8:30 A.M.: Get up, brush teeth, pick out nice tie and derby for police lineup.

9:00 A.M.: Change tape and adjust tracking in backseat camcorder.

9:15 A.M.: Drive to store, pick up more Gillette razors and Breathe-rite nasal strips.

9:45 A.M.: Take Butch Hobson's address out of Rolodex.

10:30 A.M.: Call Jerry Jones, see how that whole "Teams Police Themselves" thing is going.

12:00 noon: Enjoy a light "lunch" and make sure to hang the mirror back on the wall.

12:05 P.M.: Fifteen hundred push-ups.

1:00 P.M.: Check in at motel under the code name "Drugstore Cowboy."

2:25 P.M.: Drop by the "White House," pick up the "self-employed models."

3:18 P.M.: Call local Dallas radio station, complain about getting a bad rap.

4:30 P.M.: Stop by Cowboys practice field, make sure supply isn't being used for hash marks.

5:30 P.M.: Get home in time to watch "Absolutely Fabulous" on Comedy Central.

6:15 P.M.: Call LT for some new recipes.

7:55 P.M.: Do a few lines and forget your problems.

What the station got—and aired on television—allegedly shows Irvin buying dope. But what was more astonishing was how nonchalant he appeared on the tape, even speaking to fans as he holds what is reportedly a bag of cocaine. Michael, wake up. **WHAT PLANET ARE YOU LIVING ON?**

This belief in their own invincibility makes many athletes think they are supermen even after their careers are over. Look what happened to the Giants' Lawrence Taylor last May when he was in South Carolina to attend a golf tournament.

While he was down there, Taylor allegedly bought **$100 worth of crack** from undercover agents. Beyond the evil of crack cocaine, what makes this all so unbelievable is that Taylor reportedly just went up to a stranger on a street and made a buy, taking no more precautions then a sixteen-year-old street thug who thinks he's invincible. Lawrence, you poor, pitiful asshole.

This chronic head swell among today's athletes can be seen not just in criminal matters. Take JASON KIDD, the basketball player from UC Berkeley, who's now considered a big pro star mostly on the strength of his Nike shoe ads.

When Kidd was in college he got his coach fired because he wasn't playing enough. He had his uncle or father call the school and say, "We'll pull him out of school and your basketball program will go right down the tubes if you don't get rid of the coach." Here you have a nineteen-year-old kid and his relatives telling a university who is going to coach their basketball team. But that's **Generation X, the new breed.**

So now Kidd's been in the NBA for a couple years, he's got this big contract from Nike, and he acts like he's **God of the hardwood floor.** The shoe company chose to put a lot of their dough on this young stud, and now everybody says he's the best basketball player because he's on these flashy television commercials.

Meantime, Kidd thinks he's better than veterans like John Stockton or Gary Payton, who've been around far longer. He's not. The bottom line on Mr. Kidd is this: He can pass, but he can't shoot the fucking basketball. He couldn't shoot in college or high school, and he can't shoot now. **And by the way, his team sucks.**

The emergence of assholes like Jason Kidd is proof that we're living on a whole different sports planet now. Remember the days when athletes used to try and position their images as those of lovable giants? Remember cuddly Yogi Berra or Rosie Grier doing his *needlepoint*? Now athletes just want to market their personas as badasses.

Get the gold earring, growl like you're jacked on synthetic testosterone—hey, it's sound commercial sense now for an athlete. The public wants to associate with that badass image, and will pay for it even if it means watching their favorite sport devolve into a **trash-talking game of pigs.**

My problem with all the trash talk is that a lot of these bastards can't back it up with their play. I always loved **Muhammad Ali** because he could always back up his chatter with deeds. But a lot of today's athletes have nothing to their games *but* trash talk.

So you go see the college guys play, and they talk the talk, but their games suck. Then you go to some pro game and some schmuck is preening and jabbering on the court like he's still the badass king of the Oklahoma State field house.

To those guys I simply say **shut up and play ball.**

Still, the leagues and the advertisers who pay everybody's bills want that trash talk and intimidation because it's all evolved into a major selling point of Showtime. With an eye always watching **Madison Avenue,** league owners will generate huge revenue through television deals and ad sales. If those owners are lucky, their own sport will be deemed the hip pastime of the moment, and Spike Lee will want tickets.

The downside of all this image bullshit is that the people who run the sports have to then bend over backward for players who can do the equivalent of a 360-degree dunk. The problem is that a lot of these *glitter guys* are utter assholes. But they're also the ones who bring in the dough that keeps Showtime going.

There's even a theory going around in basketball circles right now that the time is coming when a shoe company will have a huge say in what goes down and who plays where in the NBA. Suppose, goes this theory, that one of these brash, swaggering punk basketball players is coming out of college, and say he's just

Babe's Best Bets

I predict, if the NBA season doesn't start on time, the Babe will personally:

Slap Michael Jordan . . .

Punch Patrick Ewing . . .

Step on David Stern . . .

Dunk Mugsy Bogus . . .

Decertify David Falk . . .

Make sure nobody, I mean nobody, ever goes to an NBA game again . . .

So take that, you stupid idiots. . . .

signed a contract with Nike, which I pick out only because they're the biggest shoe hucksters out there.

Anyway, suppose some flashy punk is going to be taken by the **Minnesota Timberwolves** in the first round of the NBA draft. There is a thought making the circuit among the smart guys in and around basketball that at some point in the near future the punk's shoe company might step in. They don't want their star poster boy stuck playing for some shitty team up in Minnesota or **Bumfuck, Egypt.** They want him playing in New York, or L.A., or Miami, or Orlando.

So instead, the shoe company tells their fella, "Screw Minnesota. Sit out a year, we'll pay you $20 million to do *nada,* or force them to trade you to somebody good." **HOO-WAH!**

You think this is bullshit? ***Well, then why don't you just come over here and blow me?*** I'm telling you, this is going to happen. And when it does, it's going to be the NBA's fault for letting it happen.

You know, the people who run pro basketball have gotten an awful lot of credit for having their shit together. While the idiots of the National Football League and Major League Baseball have spent much of the last decade with their thumbs up their asses, the NBA was creating and perfecting—**_Showtime._**

And Showtime, of course, is all about marketing. Look at **Michael Jordan** deciding to give up his fabulous baseball career and come back to basketball. He was floundering in the minors, a fact that was showing up on the bottom line by the fewer and fewer people who were buying Jordan's number 45 replica baseball jersey. Now that he's back in the league where he belongs, Michael is successfully selling his underpants again, and he looks like the king once more on his **McDonald's** commercials.

Advertising revenues generated, not points per game, is the ultimate yardstick for determining today's superstar. You have to be a complete brain-dead imbecile not to realize there are powers at work here greater than National Football League commissioner Paul Taglibue, baseball kingpin Bud Selig, and even the sainted basketball czar David Stern. **(A note to Saint David: Remember that even Saint Joan of Arc was ultimately burned at the stake.)**

There's even a theory going around that says Michael Jordan's to-ing and fro-ing between sports had nothing to do with his desire to play baseball. Rather, goes this supposition, Michael Jordan was actually sent into exile by the NBA for two years for his gambling activities.

Far-fetched? Maybe not. According to this theory, Jordan was suspended for two years for betting the gross national product of Paraguay on golf games and for consorting with known busted gamblers.

The way it was covered up was to let him "retire" and play baseball on a team that is owned by the same guy who owns the Chicago Bulls. It makes sense, I've got to admit, and I don't even have a problem with Michael gambling the way he liked to. If this is how he wants to relax, it's fine with me.

So now he comes back, and there's no question that **Michael Mania** has cooled down. The world isn't **"Michael Michael Michael"** anymore, and maybe that's good for him. He has more money than he'll ever need. Is that a good trade-off for never being able to go for a walk or out to a movie again? I'm not sure.

Now, when he goes to his own restaurant in Chicago, Michael Jordan has the option of sitting in a glassed-in room on the second floor, where he can stare like a goldfish in a bowl at the gawkers staring in. Or he can close the curtains around his unit, block out the locusts, and pretend he's eating in an air-raid shelter.

This is what **Showtime** has done to Michael Jordan, and maybe he's glad about it. In any case, he no longer has a choice: **Once you've gone up to celebrity Mount Olympus, there's no way down except by falling flat on your ass.**

Does the NBA even care that Showtime has completely over-shadowed the game itself? I don't think so. But they continue to take the wrong road by passing out **$40 MILLION contracts to kids just a few semesters out of high school**—the vast majority of whom will never materialize as big stars.

An even bigger sin is the influx of players into the pros straight from the twelfth grade. For every Kevin Garnett who makes it, several more will be destroyed before they ever had a chance to mature. Whether this new trend is more about need or greed, something has to be done.

When I see Glenn Robinson getting out of school and saying that if he doesn't get $100 million he's not going to play, all I want to say is a hearty **"fuck you."** Meantime, the bastards go ahead and give Robinson $76 million, to which I say, "No, fuck you!"

Unless sanity returns to all sports leagues, **they will be destroyed and taken over by shoe and soft drink companies who won't be satisfied until they man-age to sew their logos on to Michael Jordan's ass.** It's nothing but showbiz—and it's nowhere more evident than in the NBA. There, it is obvious to any Goober that the stars of the game are allowed to operate from a different rule book than their more plebeian peers (i.e., the everyday schmuck players all across the league).

A couple months ago, I took one of my producers to an

Orlando Magic game. My pal Steve hadn't covered a basketball game from courtside for a couple of years, and now he couldn't believe what he was seeing. Steve kept saying, "Oh my God, Shaq just walked and they didn't call it! Now Shaq just fouled and they didn't call that either. **What up wit' dat?"**

"Hey, Steve," I said, **"WAKE UP AND SMELL THE COFFEE,** and welcome to the new NBA. Shaq's already walked three times and fouled four times, and nothing's been called."

It was obvious. Now, I know umpires used to give Ted Williams more favorable readings on his balls and strikes just because he was **Teddy Ballgame,** but what I see in the NBA strains reality—I might as well be watching **"American Gladiators."** Shaq could have run up the floor with the basketball on his hip that night and he wouldn't have been called for traveling.

My friend Steve was outraged by the on-court double standard. All I could say to him was, **"He's Shaq.** The league doesn't want to see him foul out of the game, so he won't. Get a grip, numskull—the NBA isn't going to throw its leading stars out of the game. **It's Showtime, Bubba,** and yanking Shaq in the third quarter would be like writing Tom Cruise out of a movie with an hour left to run."

So how is it possible for a fan to remain loyal to leagues like these, filled with watered-down expansion teams run by egomaniacal puds? How can a fan pledge one's dollars and fealty to these tight-fisted asshole owners who would pull your favorite team out of your hometown in the middle of the night for the sake of the added pay toilet concession they've just been promised by the mayor of Siwash, Idaho?

But the players, too, are undeserving of love and support. How can you support teams populated by bastards who play with no more awareness or loyalty to any city beyond Hollywood? Case in point, when Shaq bolted for the bright lights of L.A. and $120 million. He's not in L.A. to play basketball but to make MUSIC VIDEOS. How can you cheer for fellas whom your daily sports page reveals to be motivated mostly by the lure of free-agency dollars, world-class drugs, and the most fetching groupies this side of Hugh Hefner's grotto? As a fan, you'd better come for the game, because otherwise you'll get your heart broken faster then you can say Walter O'Malley is alive and well and living in Art Modell's body.

A POX on all of you, players and owners, all of you!

Three
Babe's Babylon—Boxing and Other Scandals

Hi, this is the Sportsboy here, and when I think of my favorite Sports Babe memory I go back to late one night last summer. It was my birthday, and well, the Babe made me work on my birthday.

But later that night she came down into the basement and unchained me from the radiator for five minutes and let me walk around. And I got an extra helping of Spam loaf that night. . . . (Sportsboy starts crying tears of gratefulness.)

—A special Babe memory from Sportsboy on the Fabulous Sports Babe's first anniversary show, July 4, 1995

And so the Fabulous Sports Babe has begun her tome by harpooning the glamour sports for their collective lack of class and soul. I'm sure many of my more bleeding-heart fans are saying to themselves, "Yeah right, Babe, but what about *boxing?* Isn't pugilism the sleaziest sport of all?"

Well, on general principle, **my dear tree-hugging, granola-crunching, hippie asshole readers,** I must now wish you to be so good as to please go blow yourselves. You do have somewhat of a point concerning boxing's venality, you potato-headed weiners. But real life is sometimes lived in the gray area between right and wrong.

Ooh, she's fabulous!!! ♫

OK, so what do you do about the utterly corrupt world of boxing? I myself love boxing because of some prehistoric reflex embedded deep in my DNA. One of my earliest memories on this earth is of being four years old and watching "Gillette Fight Night" on the television at my Aunt Louise's house.

I sat so close to the box on fight nights that the cathode tube irradiated my hair into curls. I would watch entranced as those black and white boxers fighting on black-and-white television beat the living crap out of each other.

What up wit' dat? I wondered way back when. Boxing was *evil,* no question, but there was something about the **POWER** and **brutality** of the spectacle that wouldn't let go of my imagination. I continued to feel this way even as I grew up and realized that watching two humans destroy each other in a roped-in ring wasn't exactly how civilized people should amuse themselves.

Even today I am at times completely repulsed by the brutality and violence of boxing. And yet boxing is in some ways the ultimate sport. It is two people armed with nothing but their fists, competing in a contest where no teammate or support staff can help them.

The boxer's duty is simply to get out there and whup his challenger's ass. The only other alternative is for him to go out there and get whupped himself. Boxing is as simple, and as complicated, as that.

In a land where you need a **Ph.D. in physics to understand the infield fly rule,** there's something to be said for boxing's inherent simplicity. And I don't know why, but the Babe still gets little shivers of exhilaration every time a boxer makes his entrance to the ring with his entourage of homeboys and cut men and trainers, and maybe a girlfriend trailing behind sobbing, *"I love you,* **numbnuts***!"*

Call me old-fashioned, but that's entertainment. **HOO-WAH***!*

My all-time favorite boxer, and I know it ain't original, is **Muhammad Ali.** Even when I was a kid I loved him because of the way he ran his mouth. He reminded me of me. But even more important, Ali always backed up his words. Always. Just like me again.

I loved Ali's honesty, and I love that in any man or woman today. That Ali was willing to go to jail for five years for what he believed in was even more amazing. His religion told him not to go to war in Vietnam. His mouth told the world that "no Vietcong ever called me nigger." He escaped prison, but he gave up his title, career, and income in order to tell mainstream America to go take a flying leap—God, that took remarkable guts.

My second favorite boxer of all time is undoubtedly the great **Marvin Hagler** of Rocky Marciano's own Brockton, Massachusetts. Poor Marvin, he should have gotten a shot at the middleweight championship before he got so old, but he still did all right for himself.

I used to live on Cape Cod in the town where Marvin used to train. You'd get up in the morning and see Marvin running up and down the dunes, then you'd come home late at night and he'd still be running, running, running. I never saw a body so sculpted as Marvin's; he was unquestionably the best conditioned person I'd ever seen.

Of course, he wasn't famous for having the brightest bulb in his head. I have a friend, Virginia, who once went to see Marvin spar during an exhibition at his training camp one Halloween. She asked him to inscribe a picture with greetings of the day, and Marvin Hagler agreed—and then asked her how to spell "Virginia" and "Halloween."

All right, all right, calm down out there you ignorant bastards, I'm getting to the present. What about **Mike Tyson?** I've taken an awful lot of shit from uninformed airheads for putting Tyson on my program, and now I will state my case. I'm not here to defend what he did—for that is indefensible. Rather, I just want to say that Mike Tyson has the right to make his living, no matter what crimes he has done—and paid for—in the past.

I think that Mike Tyson is an interesting character in a dirty world. That said, I also believe that Mike Tyson did everything he was charged with in the rape of that young woman. I think he raped her, and I was **100 percent** for his going to jail. But last time I checked, Mike Tyson served every second of his sentence, without one day off for good behavior. He served his time, and now I believe it's time to let him move on.

It can also be instructive, you who are quick to hang fools, to consider Tyson's inner reality. Here's a guy who grew up believing that the greatest thing he could ever dream of becoming was the heavyweight boxing champion of the world. For other people the greatest aspiration could be to become a doctor or a priest, but Mike Tyson was born and bred to destroy people, and to dream of doing just that all the way to the heavyweight belt. And Tyson was good at fucking people up, in the street or in the ring.

All his life, Mike Tyson was told he was the greatest. And then, after he won the heavyweight belt, the line of people who wanted him, or at least a piece of him, would have reached all the way to Uranus.

Of course, every woman seemed to want Mike Tyson. Tyson had probably never experienced a woman whom he wanted rejecting him. Now again, in no way did that young woman deserve what happened. There was some weird shit going on in there, what with Tyson calling her "mommy" over and over on the bed. In his own mind, Tyson probably thought she was just playing hard to get, not that he was raping her.

But he was raping her, and it was important for that trial to be played out in the open as it was. People need to understand what date rape is. The country needed it explained that she didn't want what he wanted, she said no, and Mike Tyson got his ass dragged to prison.

But he served his time.

Soon after Tyson got out of prison he came on "The Fabulous Sports Babe Show." At the end of the interview, Tyson said, *"I love you, Babe."* And I said, *"I love you too, Mike."* And within another microsecond the phone lines in the studio were flaming with people accusing me of going soft on Tyson simply because he could knock out any mother on the planet. I wasn't.

For some reason I can't quite pinpoint or explain, I'm able to separate in this one instance the athlete and his crime. I can't do that with other people, and I'm really harsh on athletes, but Tyson is different. He most certainly needed to go to jail—and yet I still felt compelled to spend an hour last night watching the video *Mike Tyson's Greatest Hits.*

I'm not ashamed for enjoying Mike Tyson's work, although many have said I should be. To them I say, ***"Excuse me, I've got my own opinion."*** The athlete-criminals whom I do have a problem with, however, are the ones who don't serve their time. Like Lawrence Phillips from the proud campus of the University of Nebraska.

Babe's Best Bets

The Babe is predicting that Jim Nantz and Terry Donahue will never work another football game, but they will be paired as bumbling announcers on CBS's new Bill Cosby sitcom.

The Babe predicts that **Tom Osborne** will reconsider his decision and will now suspend **Lawrence Phillips** for six months—effective immediately.

And the Babe is prediciting that Steve Spurrier will protest last night's Fiesta Bowl loss, claiming that the Nebraska defense rushed Danny Wuerffel before counting to five Mississippi.

So what, said the wise men of Nebraska, if Phillips hideously assaulted his ex-girlfriend last fall. Mr. Phillips, a first-round draft pick this year of the St. Louis Rams, pleaded no contest to the charges and was kept on the Nebraska team by Coach Tom Osborne, who said the young man needed the structure and competition of football to deal with his difficult times. **WAKE UP, Tom—what price success, you dirtbag?**

But there was more going on in Nebraska recently than the heartwarming story of Lawrence Phillips's rehabilitation. Let us not forget Christian Peter, the Cornhuskers football player who just got arrested, also for assaulting a woman. Christian, as it were, was also slated to be a first-round NFL draft pick next year.

Almost. Picked in the next round by the New England Patriots, Peter was quickly dropped by the Pats when local fans and feminists made so much mess for the team that they had to let Christian go free. Of course, the National Football League will never take a stand on such criminals/players. *Their silence, in essence, says that because you are a football player it's OK to beat up women.*

Meantime, women assaulted in football factory towns like Lincoln, Nebraska, are pressured not to testify against athletes. If they do, they're warned, they'll be drummed out of town for fucking up the career of one of the campus's big football stars.

And even when these women keep quiet they are punished. Take the woman who was beaten up by Lawrence Phillips—she had her basketball scholarship taken away by Nebraska because of, said the *New York Times,* "a lack of progress in her play." Never mind that she'd earned a spot on the Big 8 academic honor roll last year—for shame.

These scandals at Nebraska will **taint Coach Tom Osborne forever, as they should.** The regents at that school, who care only about how their football team is ranked and not the safety of students, are a disgrace to higher education.

The ultimate proof of an athlete criminal literally getting away with murder, of course, is **O. J. Simpson.** That lying, murdering bastard actually had the gall to call my office and leave a message saying that he would like to appear on my show. *Yeah right, O.J., the day I let a lying, murdering bastard like you on my show is the moment when monkeys begin to fly out of my ass.*

I couldn't believe that trial. And if I have one lesson to give the boys and girls of America about justice in this country, it would be that we live in a sexist society. If we didn't, how could it be that O. J. Simpson cuts off the head of the mother of his children, murders Ron Goldman, and gets to skate away free?

```
Hey Babe—
Did you hear about O.J.'s
new limousine service?

It guarantees getting you
to the airport with an
hour to kill!!!
```

Meanwhile, Hollywood madame Heidi Fleiss is given three years for her assorted crimes. How can this be? Yet there, in a twisted nutshell holding Heidi and O.J., is what's wrong with this country today.

Now perhaps some of you numbnuts feel I am being too hard on O.J., **THAT LYING, MURDERING BASTARD.** In my defense, I've tried to understand his side, I really have. It's just that I feel it is important to me to point out certain things to those assholes who call the show and say, "Lighten up on O.J., he was a great runner."

My standard response has been, "I know he was a great running back, you idiot. ***And did you forget he also cut off his wife's head?"***

I did try on "The Fabulous Sports Babe Show" to get at the real issues and deeper truths behind the O. J. Simpson trial. I even had a show where I asked that only African-Americans call in, and that they try to explain to me why they didn't think O.J. did it. I told my listeners up front that I thought **O.J. did it hook, line, and sinker.** And I'm also convinced that the bastard thought he could murder everybody in sight and get away with it just because he was a football hero.

The call-in response that day was very interesting. One African-American woman called and said, "I feel like I have to defend the entire race at all times." No you don't, I told her, and I believe that.

Another guy called in and said that I could just never understand the situation from a black perspective. I got royally pissed off at that. "Why can't I understand?" I asked him. "Just because I'm essentially a suburban white chick, I can't comprehend the facts of the O. J. Simpson case?"

"You just don't *understand*," he continued, at which point I cut him off. "**Fuck you, buddy,**" I said. "I *do* understand."

Babe's Best Bets

I predict the singer formerly known as Prince will sue Mark Fuhrman when he learns Fuhrman not only hit on Vanity, but Shelia E. and Apollonia, too.

That case had more than just a retelling of Shakespeare's *Othello* going for it. It also provided a mirror for everything that is wrong with American society, let alone sports. It was an important lesson in twisted civics, and every day during the case "The Fabulous Sports Babe Show" utilized two reporters from Court TV to sum up the scene for my listeners. Despite the fact that I run a sports show, I felt it was also important to have Geraldo Rivera and Larry King, the two leading scholars of the case, on the show to discuss its many complexities.

Sadly, O. J. Simpson is far from being the only athlete allowed to walk away after his crimes threatened his career. Looking the other way is simply the way it's always been done in professional sports, especially when it comes to drug use.

True, baseball players getting wasted is a tradition older than the seventh-inning stretch. Ever since *The Sporting News* reported in the 1880s that St. Louis Browns outfielder Curt Welch habitually hid cases of beer behind the billboards lining Sportsman's Park, it has been common knowledge that baseball players enjoyed getting high before, after, and sometimes during games. In 1903 a

Cincinnati newspaper went so far as to publish the following advice to the city's constantly drunk Reds: "Whenever a ball looks like this—000—take a chance on the middle one." **HOO-WAH!**

Later, **Babe Ruth** and **Mickey Mantle** did much of their best work either plastered or hung over. Pete Rose admitted he used to enjoy an occasional pregame upper; pitcher Dock Ellis even said he was tripping on acid when he threw a no-hitter for the Pittsburgh Pirates in 1970. **What up wit' dat, Dock?**

And still, few lessons have been learned. Look at the apparently revitalized **Doc Gooden,** who pitched that amazing no-hitter for the Yankees early in the '96 season. He was able to get away with so much drug snorting and gun-lugging behavior as a Met simply because he walked the walk and talked the talk of a real hero.

Bullshit. Even Doc's drug counselors were able to rationalize what was actually going on with their meal ticket. Gooden has even been quoted as saying he would drink in front of his drug counselors when he was supposedly recovering from cocaine abuse. "Don't get me wrong, it's not like I had their permission," Gooden said. "No one ever said, 'As long as you're drinking and not drugging it's OK.' But I was still the patient. I was still sick."

And he never had to pay the price until it was almost too late. So you want to bitch to me about how I can go so easy on Mike Tyson? **Have you ever heard the notion of paying one's debt to society?**

Tyson the boxer, meantime, remains a master. I went to his first fight against that *fainting weiner boy* Peter McNeely just because I wanted to see the return. I watched him pummel Lennox Lewis, taking the big guy out in three rounds. For every second of that fight, I was amazed by his ability to shove it up the ass of all the people who said Mike Tyson had lost his speed. The man-beast is most definitely back.

One of the pieces of evidence used to support the notion that Tyson is an utter idiot is that as soon as he got out of prison he said that he was going to cast his lot with Don King, whom he called the greatest promoter in the world. In this case, I think Iron Mike was right.

Jesus God Almighty, how can so many geeks find my phone number!!#?!

Now there are many things you can say about Don King, the man **whose hair is even more fabulous than mine— barely.** Yes, he once beat a man to death. Yes, he ripped off a stable of fighters for the lion's share of their winnings. Yes, he used up, and then sold out, Muhammad Ali.

Many people say Don King is a complete sewer rat, but boxing fans everywhere would be wise to remember what a sad state of affairs boxing would be in if not for Don King. The **"sweet science of bruising,"** as some dipshit Brit termed it three hundred years ago, would be dead without King. Only he can consistently make the matches, build the hype, and pull off the hocus-pocus that makes even the most casual of boxing fans check the newspaper every once in a while.

As with Tyson, however, I'm not excusing any of the bullshit Don King pulls in his quest to build his own plantation on the backs of his fighters. Still, we somehow expect this in the world of boxing—the science of **"trickeration"** is what Don King calls it, while others just say **"lying."**

All in all, I try not to excessively judge a sport that everybody already knows is sleazy. Selfishly, I like Don King because he's always a great guest on the show, one who's never afraid to be completely wack. Don King has always been a courteous and fun guest, and he always brings his own fireworks. And then, of course, there's that soothing, relaxing voice of his. Anyway, dear moralizers, I'd be the biggest idiot in the world not to want Don King on my show—and I'm not just saying this because he likes to put Mike Tyson on the phone whenever we chat.

Mike, of course, never speaks to the media, who continue to portray him as a **psychopathic hybrid of King Kong and Adolf Hitler.** He certainly ain't no choirboy—but the trail of misdeeds I know of perpetrated by squeaky clean–looking white athletes would straighten even Don King's hair.

Once upon a time, Mike Tyson was sold to America as a role model. If you recall, Mike Tyson's commercial peak occurred before he looked like a lobotomized inpatient from *One Flew Over the Cuckoo's Nest* on Barbara Walters's show, prior to his raping a teenager. Before all that, Madison Avenue thought Tyson might even be able to hawk Pepsi. So they dressed Mike Tyson up and had him smile nice for the cameras while holding up a can of soda.

Back then, Mike Tyson was sold as the kind of tame and gentle giant whom a Desiree Washington could safely follow into his hotel room. Maybe we'd all be better if we didn't expect our heroes to be as shiny and wholesome as a Wheaties box. *If you need strangers to look up to, you need to get a job, get a haircut, get a fucking life!*

Me, I prefer to remain objective about an athlete's felonies and their relation to his game. Last season, I can't tell you how much I wanted in my heart of hearts for the FLORIDA GATORS to win the national football title by beating those woman-assaulting Nebraska Cornhuskers. But one of the reasons I'm able to remain objective better than most people is that I'm able to understand football apart from the personalities. So while I may feel with my heart, I always rely on my brain for the correct information.

And that is how I knew that no football team on the planet was going to beat those sleazebag **Nebraska Pigfuckers** with all their multitalent felons and assaulters. Knowing that Nebraska couldn't be beaten didn't make me like them any better, hell no. **Do you think I wanted Lawrence Phillips, *this woman-beating, insane bastard*, and his teammates to be champs?**

Of course I didn't want that to happen. But the fact remains that Nebraska was a machine of a football team, and you simply couldn't take that away from them. But while we're ignoring athlete thugs on campus, why are we also paying so much attention to players not standing during the playing of *"The Star-Spangled Banner"*? I mean, who cares if an athlete does or doesn't rise during the national anthem? As a matter of fact, why do we need to play that song before each and every sporting event? It's not written in the Constitution, for God's sake, that we must listen to Francis Scott Key before watching men run around in shorts.

Is this why we go to sporting events, to see how patriotic the jocks are who happen to be wearing the home colors of the city we happen to live in? And yet players standing for the anthem keeps coming back as this big **chest-thumping** issue for these redneck hosebags.

Standing for the national anthem came up most recently in Denver, when Mahmoud Abdul-Rauf of the Denver Nuggets was suspended because he refused to stand and honor the flag when "The Star-Spangled Banner" was tootled. Mahmoud is a Muslim, and he says that his religion teaches that God comes before the flag of any nation. The Nuggets dealt with the situation by recently trading him to Sacramento.

That's what he believes, and because of that, in my book and in this book, he's automatically right. If I remember correctly from my sixth-grade American history class, we live in a nation built on a foundation of religious tolerance. Please write me in care of the Airstream if I'm wrong, but isn't Abdul-Rauf allowed to believe in something even if the majority—**that means you, o ignorant rednecks**—thinks he should be tied to a stake, covered with honey, then eaten alive by poisonous ants?

The whole hypocrisy of this issue makes the Fabulous Sports

Babe feel **A NOT SO FABULOUS HEAT RASH.** For twenty years there have been guys not standing for the anthem. Usually they've been Jehovah's Witnesses, and most often they just stay in the locker room for the pregame festivities.

Lou Whitaker, a superb player for the Detroit Tigers, always stayed in the locker room when "The Star-Spangled Banner" was sung. So what? Who cares? Hey, you Bubbas out there who think that this country is all about everyone thinking just like you— excuse me, **but would you please be so polite as to honorably go take the gas pipe?**

Instead of concentrating on this burning issue, might patriots not be better off combating the much more pressing problem of athletes beating and assaulting women and then getting away with it? I find it so ironic that in a day and age when athletes are supposedly so much **badder** and **tougher** and **meaner** than ever, you almost never hear about jocks getting in fights like they used to. You remember, the kind of fight where men battled other men.

Remember how you used to read about athletes getting into fights in bars and strip joints with civilians who'd spit on, insulted, threatened, or challenged them? The classic case of this kind of manly behavior was Billy Martin's most famous bar bout. His opponent that night was Joseph Cooper, who identified himself to the baseball manager as the **"Marshmallow King"** before beginning to heckle Martin in a hotel lobby in Minnesota. Billy Martin punched the marshmallow man into twenty stitches, and promptly lost his job.

Now you never hear about athletes fighting guys anymore. No, **all you ever read about is jocks beating up women.** *What up wit' dat?*

Maybe these modern athletes are even bigger **pussies** than we ever suspected. I know for a fact that guys with chips on their shoulders still seek out jocks in order to challenge them with lines like, "You're not so tough. I'm going to kick your ass, Mr. All Pro." Why don't players ever take these assholes up on their offers? Wouldn't that be more manly than smacking around their girlfriends and wives?

The most noted case of not copping to your responsibility in the last few years, however, must certainly be **PETE ROSE.** I don't begrudge Pete his caveman attitude toward women: Besides his legendary affinity for groupies in every Major League city, who could ever forget his comment on how to end a marriage? "Hey, just give her a million bucks and tell her to hit the road," Rose told *Sports Illustrated.* **Fine, Pete, whatever.**

What I can't stand is his saying that he was railroaded by **Faye Vincent,** the former commissioner of baseball. As far as I'm concerned, Faye Vincent is a good and honorable man. And Faye Vincent told me on the show that Pete Rose bet on baseball. *Pete Rose knows he did it, Faye said, and I know it.*

From my learned perspective, **PETE ROSE SHOULD NOT BE IN THE HALL OF FAME IF HE BET ON BASE-BALL.** I know people say it shouldn't matter, that the guy had the hits and deserves to go in. Now if he'd drank or drugged his way out of baseball, I'd agree that he should go in. He's only hurting himself.

But betting on baseball could easily tear at the very fabric of the game. Certainly this kind of gambling has a much greater potential to destroy baseball than the combined effects of cocaine and groupies ever have. These latter sins only harm the individual; betting on games affects an entire team.

What really *gets my underwear in a bunch* (I know that excites you Bubbas, but calm down) is that Pete Rose has never stood up and said, "I did this and I'm sorry." Instead, Rose has always walked around with his "Hit King" hat on saying that he got railroaded and that Commissioner Bart Giamatti, who pushed the investigation before his sudden tragic death, was a fat pig who deserved to die.

The fact is that Pete Rose isn't getting shafted. Why would some old man commissioner who was president of Yale want to fuck him? Bart Giamatti's life and world were bigger than that. Pete Rose should open his eyes, pay some public penance, and maybe, just maybe, he'll get into the Hall of Fame someday.

These scandals, of course, are the famous fuckups that everybody knows about. But every sports reporter worth his clogged arteries also knows of dozens of little miniscandals and horrific situations involving athletes that never see print. Even today, the gentlemen's agreement of **"at all costs don't wreck**

somebody's career" remains in full effect in many quarters inhabited by male sportswriters.

In 1985, for example, the Redskins and Raiders came to Tampa for the Superbowl. A friend of mine owned a bar there, and the night before the game John Riggins came in, got drunk, and played the next day. Fine, nothing new there in professional football. But what was most definitely different about that pregame drinking bout occurred when Riggins, wearing an air force flight suit, unzipped himself and placed his dick on the bar. **HOO-WAH!**

"Get that thing off of there!" my friend behind the bar ordered, which Riggins did. *God bless America!*

Steroids were another largely secret issue, especially in the early 1980s when no one knew anything about the long-term effects of the muscle-building drugs. Still, it was remarkable back in those days to see the changes that came over athletes in an amazingly short period of time.

Even this monkey on my back has more integrity and smarts than most of the stone lying, cheating, obnoxious losers in Major League sports!

During one off-season, a Tampa running back went from looking like an ordinary Joe to a cross between **ARNOLD SCHWARZENEGGER AND THE MICHELIN MAN.** From first impressions, it looked as if he had swallowed an air hose. He was a completely different human being, as well as an utter idiot. The guy couldn't even lift weights because he had gotten so bulked up in a few months.

Still, the weirdest enzyme reaction I ever saw involved **Punkin' Williams,** a Bucs running back from several years ago. Punkin' wasn't taking drugs; he was simply completely out of shape for football training camp.

Punkin' had apparently not worked out over the winter, because when he ran wind sprints during training camp he threw up every time he made a ten-yard turn. We had to be careful as reporters, because if we didn't watch it, Williams would be soiling our shoes every ten seconds.

After a few rounds of this performance, the gathered sportswriters finally gave our gastronomically challenged players a new name. Ladies and gentlemen, may I present you with Pukin' Punkin' Williams!

Now, that's entertainment!

Four
The Babe's Baby

Behind the Scenes at
"The Fabulous Sports Babe Show"
(The Art of Handling Callers)

As I like to say, my show is a party where everyone is invited. But, and this is a significant caveat, you must wear a helmet when you come into my arena. Many callers to my show forget this rule, and their failure to pay attention reflects upon them as the unbelievable **idiots** they truly are.

I still remember running into a multiple-time caller one spring when I was attending an NBA playoff game in Seattle. I'm sitting there at my usual courtside perch when all of a sudden some **tree-hugging, granola-chomping Seattle hippie** comes up to me and grabs me by my forearm. This bastard is six feet tall with long stringy hair, and he's really pissed off.

"You bitch!" he yells at me. "You hung up on me four times on the radio!"

I was neither amused nor frightened. I just leaned into his face and said, "So why did you call back the other three times, you dope? Why, if you take this so seriously, do you keep calling back? Don't you realize that our entire audience is laughing at the assholes like you who take this all seriously? Don't you realize, you moron, that this is the joke of the entire show? That you, in particular, are the joke?"

How **stupid** *are my callers?* Well, 50 percent of the people who think I hung up on them in the middle of our conversation were not hung up on. I'm always trying to get as many opinions as possible into every show, which means I'm very into getting callers to quickly make their point and then move on.

Unlike many talk radio hosts, I have no interest in sitting

around killing airtime by saying to my callers, *Are you sure you're done now? Is there anything else you'd like to say?* I just hang up when a caller's point has been made, and there's no disrespect intended. If you understand this is how "The Fabulous Sports Babe Show" works, then you're fine.

Still, I feel I must admit that I automatically assume that anybody who calls my program is an idiot. Who, after all, would call up a radio station to chat? **What kind of person would waste their life dialing talk show hosts?** I've never once felt compelled to call a talk show and blabber. And I only have one friend, a lawyer, who bothers to call sports radio talk shows. His on-air moniker is the Barrister, and his hobby is pissing off talk show hosts with his well-honed debating skills.

Sally Jessy Raphael, for one, had a different approach than me when she took calls. I've noticed that Sally began by assuming all of her callers were sane, not freaks. She made the erroneous assumption that these morons calling her were rational, reasonable people, and that everybody they were bitching about was entirely at fault.

Well, **FUCK YOU**, **Sally,** I've made the exact opposite assumption about my callers. Unlike you, I've decided that everyone who calls me is the **enemy.** I assume they are all nuts, and once in a while I'm pleasantly surprised to learn that not everybody who calls a radio station is an utter bedbug.

Now, if callers to the Babe show have their shit together, I'm happy to talk to them on the air. Still, some people don't understand how I can hang up on someone after two seconds without hearing them out. I hang up on these people, I explain, because I just know. I've been under these headphones for almost twenty years, and I know instantly where virtually every call is going. If I cut a caller off it's because I sensed in my soul of souls that this guy was either going to bore us; give us some shaggy dog, never-ending bullshit story; or try and say "fuck" on the air. **HOO-WAH**!

This is where the **genius** of **Sportsboy** comes through. Denis the Sportsboy, the latest incarnation of my famous slave and assistant, also serves as the show's official call screener. DENIS IS BRILLIANT AT THE ART, a fact that comes as no surprise to me.

I unchained Sports-boy long enough for him to actually fly this plane at the NBA finals this year. I truly am a kind and benevolent ruler.

Because Denis is, in fact, an utter asshole, he is easily able to screen out the calls of other assholes trying to break into my show via the phone lines. Denis the Sportsboy knows these demented fruitcakes, and he understands them. Indeed, one of the main reasons I keep Sportsboy is because he is a true idiot. **He is a buffoon, and thereby knows the Babe's natural enemies.** Denis thrives on my staff because he truly is one of them.

People are always asking me why we have so many fewer asshole callers on my program than on any other sports talk show. The reason is that we screen so intensely and make sure we don't have **Lame Joe** from **Nowhere, Ohio,** getting on the air. Sometimes we put these guys on just to be amused, but everybody working here knows that with so many millions of dollars riding on this show, we can't have shitty phone calls chewing up our time.

To achieve this we go far deeper in our call screening process than any other sports radio talk show. Indeed, it's more like a proctological exam than a normal sifting process. A lot of people will call up other programs and tell the screener, "I want to talk about baseball," and boom, they're on. Not on "The Fabulous Sports Babe Show."

Here in the Airstream, would-be callers might say they want to talk about the Yankees, and Sportsboy will immediately demand of them, ***"What about the Yankees?"*** The listener might then say, **"Their relief pitching." "What about their relief pitching?"** Sportsboy will say. ***"Which relievers do you want to talk about?"*** Sportsboy's inquiry will go five or six questions deep as he determines if the caller can contribute to the show.

The point of this is to make sure this guy knows of what he speaks. And also that he's living in this century. I don't want some sixty-year-old calling up to talk about the rich legacy of Toe Blake or the days when real football players tussled without face masks. It's GOOD-BYE AND GILLOOLY to any caller when they start talking like that. Sixty-year-olds are welcome to call my show, but they can't expect I'll ever allow them to delve into that Goober bullshit.

Our program's vigorous screening process also allows us to weed out jerk-offs who just want to scream obscenities on the air so they can play the tape to their fellow jerk-off friends. These people are assholes, which is why it's perfect luck for us that Sportsboy is just a total asshole himself.

My Sportsboy is truly the biggest asshole on the planet, and he's not afraid to give it back when he's confronted by the voice of some schmuck trying to score points with their buddies via my show. "Fuck you!!" he says, hanging up on his own species.

So for a lot of these callers, it's just hello and good-bye. The days of callers meandering through a talk show are over. There is a new sheriff in town, and she decides when you're done. Entering the arena with me is your exercise in **Babe-ocracy**. And if you fail the test, don't go crying and bitching to me when you see me at some basketball game. No one told you to call.

On "The Fabulous Sports Babe Show," I'm on guard against more than just your run-of-the-mill sports assholes. One of the best things about my job is that it gives the Babe, in her own inim-

Sportsboy,
the biggest
asshole on
the planet,
and my agent,
Lisa Miller,
plotting at
Babeworld.

itable way, a forum in which to fight the hatred and idiocy that permeates the world.

Now Listen Up, Assholes

Magic Johnson contracting the AIDS virus, I thought, was an important goddamn issue to explore in depth. And I'm not just talking about Magic in tabloid terms, but in a manner that might actually make it possible for some of my listeners with sawdust for brains to understand the gravity of the illness. It's good to talk not only about the disease, I decided, but also about people's phobias about it.

I think it's important that everyone listening to my show understand that **AIDS IS ABOUT MUCH MORE THAN JUST AN INFECTIOUS DISEASE.** It's also about homophobia. It's about people not understanding the rights of others to be different. It's about spreading hate through bad information.

Santa Babe!

The brilliant Babe-aholic Tom Mollica, chronicler of my fabulousness.

I told you I could play!

So when some dope calls up with some idiotic insight about Magic, I'll make a judgment call as to whether the depth of his ignorance might be instructive. I'm so good at what I do, **my**

Even Tom can barely squeeze me into the Airstream.

beloved Bubbas, that I can easily tell what some dickweed is up to light-years before even he knows.

Still, people will say, "Why did you cut that caller off so early?" I just tell them I have a magic sense of who's an asshole. God granted me the gift of knowing immediately who is going to try and say nasty words on the air. They can't fool me, those assholes, because I've been doing this my whole life. I am the all-knowing **Madame Rolonda,** I can tell where every caller is going. I know if they're trying to make a point that makes sense or just trying to mess with me.

I also don't like religious fanatic callers who haven't learned the notion that God, if she exists, has a sense of humor. I recently heard from a listener who said that I was being sacrilegious every time I played our "Friday Song," a tune using the melody of the ***HALLELUJAH* chorus.** Hey, buddy, give me a break.

Of course, I don't let any of these **Fantasy Football or**

Rotisserie Baseball assholes anywhere near my show. Who needs them? Other fantasy assholes—and there are a lot of them—will listen to some statistics pud talking on the radio. But these are not the people I want listening to or appearing on my show, because the woman listening to the radio on her way to an appointment or the guy listening while he sorts mail at the post office will immediately click to FM if they hear stats bullshit. They don't want to hear it—they'd rather hear music, or a personality as *effervescent* as the Fabulous Sports Babe.

It's interesting where I draw my loyal listeners from. For most people who listen to my show, their second preference isn't some other talk radio program, but an FM rock station. This is a hip room I play to, mostly eighteen- to thirty-four-year-olds with some taste, so I'm not going to poison their listening pleasure with filler and crappy calls. When I started in talk radio I was just glad to get anybody to call me, so I'd let any asshole talk. No longer.

I must admit, however, that sometimes I'm surprised by people I thought at first were morons. Once, during the baseball strike, Sportsboy put through a caller for some reason who sounded just like one more redneck asshole. It turned out that this fellow was the guy who opened the parking lot gate for the baseball players at the Atlanta baseball stadium, where he was paid something like $3.50 an hour. Yawn, right?

No. *I actually kept him on for five minutes, which for me is one step away from a marriage proposal.* It was a nice bit; I asked him how he felt opening the gate so the players could get their Beamers and Mercedes out of the lot. He talked about how the players never even said hello to him once. Apparently he'd say "good morning" every day, and they'd just walk on by.

The car parker's spiel was very powerful radio, a real statement on class distinctions. It was enlightening to hear about these selfish *prima donna ballplayers* refusing to even acknowledge this guy getting paid at Arby's rates. Whoever he was, this guy was a great caller.

There is no question that some of the most screwed up calls we've ever received on the show were also among the most entertaining. Wrong numbers dialed into our switchboard can be hys-

Lenny the
Phone Freak—
this weasel
always has a
phone glued to
his face. What
a jerk!

terical, especially when I play along with the unfortunate misdialing sap.

One of my best examples came last year when **Lenny the Phone Freak,** a.k.a. Len Weiner, the show's original producer, was manning the phones. On this particular day, a woman called and asked the Freak, "Is this the Psychic Hotline?"

Lenny knew we'd hit gold. "Yes, yes it is," he told the woman. Then he came through my headphones and asked, "Is this the Psychic Hotline?"

"Of course," I told Lenny. "Let's go." And here is the total, unexpurgated, shameless, heard on-air dialogue.

BABE: Who is this?

CALLER: Margaret.

BABE: Hi Margaret, who you calling?

CALLER: The psychic, Madame Elaine.

BABE: Oh, you've come to the right place. This is Madame Rolonda, Lane's on her coffee break. What's on your mind, dear?

CALLER: I'm having problems with my . . . I'll call him my husband. I want to know if he's for real.

BABE: Does he look real?

CALLER: I've been trying to help him with his house.

BABE: What's the matter with his house, hon?

CALLER: He had some homeless people in his house, and they kind of messed it up.

BABE: I knew that.

CALLER: Hello?

BABE: We're here, we're just waiting to feel your pain. We want to feel it. We also want you to take all your money and bet it on the lottery with these numbers.

CALLER: OK.

BABE: Seven, fourteen, twenty-two, and nine. That will be twenty-five bucks, OK? Hang on the line and give us your credit card.

CALLER: OK.

AH, THE DRAMA OF GOOD RADIO, HUH?

I've had a number of feuds with entire cities on my show, and I enjoy these campaigns mightily. There is nothing that gets the Babe's airstream juices flowing as smoothly and strongly as a grudge match with some so-called metropolis filled with ignorant dipshits who think I've disrespected their team, city, or honor. Why don't all you hale and swell fellows bent on revenge for the Babe please venture over to my corner and be so civilized as to blow me?

The interesting thing about all the noise these **yo·yos** make is that I don't have to try very hard to show the audience what losers these people really are. All I need to do as a radio host is to allow these ignorant assholes to hang themselves with their own words.

One of my more noted blood revenge campaigns was waged against the ***louts* of Columbus, Ohio,** home of the Ohio State Buckeyes, the ghost of Woody Hayes, and the most idiotic out-patients masquerading as fans in the world. The war between me and OSU supporters began a couple years ago when a group of ignorant pea-brains began campaigning to fire **COACH JOHN COOPER** after he went 10–0–1 for the season.

Ohio State football coach John Cooper—I love the guy!

The tie, sad to say for Coach Cooper, was with Michigan. In Columbus, these OSU fans are so obsessed in thinking that the world begins and ends with Ohio State football that they begin acting oddly. They think that a half-blemish on their record perpe-trated by OSU's archrival—a tie with Michigan!—is reason to tar and feather and stick the old pigskin up the ass of a fine and decent man who also happens to be a helluva football coach. The even odder thing about all this is that almost all of the flak was coming

Can you tell which one isn't part of the John Cooper family?

at John Cooper from people in Ohio who had never attended that university.

Bastards from hell, they wouldn't know a good football coach if he came up in the stands and blew them. So of course I gave these OSU partisans the righteous business on my show for being such unrefined idiots. Meantime, back in Columbus, the goobers were being egged on to wage war upon me by some local radio talk show hosts who were just as ignorant as the fans.

This was uncalled-for **bullshit.** It was nothing less than a crime that my show's phone lines were suddenly unavailable to my fine and cultured listeners who wished to discuss the physics of the curveball and the deeper literary meanings of Joyce Carol Oates's book on boxing.

These meek heavy-thinkers are people who need their spokesperson too, and it was for them that I refused to be bullied by those **dirtbag Ohio State fanatics.** I'm sure you know the kind—the people who think America would be a much better place today if Woody Hayes had only been given an army in Vietnam.

My next step in the War on the Idiots was easy and crushing to the opposition. Mark Mason, the general manager of ESPN

Radio, simply called the program director of the Columbus Babe franchise.

Our guy told their guy that if that station didn't knock it off and stop encouraging OSU fans to swamp the lines of our show, they would lose "The Fabulous Sports Babe Show" forever. We would switch the show to one of their competitors and simply kick their asses. We've done this before when an affiliate acts up— we simply go elsewhere in their market.

"Never mind," said our sudden new friends in Columbus, sounding more like Emily Littella from "Saturday Night Live" than the fearsome, chest-thumping Buckeye fans of lore. And nothing more was heard. Now my ratings are huge in Columbus. **HOO-WAH!**

All this, of course, was planned by me as part of my fiendish plot to forge a ratings-rich **Global Babe Network.** Columbus, like everywhere else, fell for the Babe's act! I make listeners and radio hosts talk about me. Even if they hate me, they will surely be shortly suffering from an advanced case of Babe-aholism. My dupes, I tell you, and my enemies are the easiest to capture.

Next year, the shit will be flying from someplace else. It all makes for great theater and terrific radio. All you have to do is get these civic booster bastards whining and crying, and soon the

Babe Flashback

On February 7, 1903, in a regulation baseball game played at Columbus, Ohio, the Indians beat the New York Highlanders 9–2. The game was played in Columbus because of Sunday restrictions in Cleveland.

And just in case you didn't know it: The players hated Columbus so much, the Sunday restrictions were abolished in Cleveland and a new restriction was immediately passed prohibiting any professional sports event from taking place in Columbus again.

whole country will be saying, "Who are all these assholes in that city?"

Sadly, you find this weird, small-town mentality in cities much, much bigger than **Nowhere, Ohio.** Take my old hometown of Seattle, a burg I spent some significant time trying to pull into the twentieth century. In Seattle, people don't believe anything happens in the world past Mount Rainier.

They were blinded to the fact that there's this whole wide world out there that doesn't give a shit that the Seahawks have won two straight. **"What up wit' dis city?"** I kept asking on my local radio show at KJR, my last job before coming to ESPN. Every other radio jockey in town at that time was complaining on the air about me dogging their beloved town. They all wanted to know what I thought I was doing. These competing voices got an unbelievable number of people to turn me on just to see what all the buzz was about.

Once those listeners punched my station, it was my job to keep them. And I did, with my inimitable and heartwarming style. *Not!* But I love it when my competitors or blocs of fans complain about me, my message, or my style.

The most recent example of this phenomenon of entire towns losing their minds over a sports team was the **Kansas City Chiefs** and their fans in the 1995 football season. People across the country couldn't wait for the Chiefs to have their asses handed back to them in the playoffs, and it wasn't because of the team.

Rather, it was because those idiot fans got the idea in their heads that because the Chiefs went 13–3 they were the greatest football team since the 1928 Canton Bulldogs. With that, Kansas City fans suddenly became more obnoxious then a national Shriners' convention.

They kept calling my show by the thousands in order to bluster about how Kansas City would destroy Pittsburgh in the playoffs, and then how the Chiefs would kick the Cowboys' asses in the Super Bowl. At first, I would just mildly point out to these Kansas City fans that their team had compiled their impressive record against opponents with a worse winning percentage than the Italian army. The Chiefs' record was make-believe, I told them, pure phony baloney.

So don't be blinded by the glow of newfound apparent success, I wisely advised the Chiefs fans. Do not go around trash-talking about how the Chiefs will obliterate the Steelers and Cowboys. But then, like their numskull residents, entire cities get furious when you question their critical judgment.

Soon I was getting constant calls from **human vegetables** screaming at me that "you don't give our team any respect." Now when listeners hear that phrase uttered by a caller on a sports talk show—"we don't get any respect"—they automatically know that they're hearing some small-town nobody with an inflated sense of civic importance. These whining jerkoffs puff up their chests and preen. They complain about how their team is "disrespected," and they make complete asses out of themselves. ***Please call "The Fabulous Sports Babe Show" and let me put you in your proper places!***

Jesus, respect. When fans lay that **"respect"** bullshit on me, everybody else listening in the country automatically hates them. This is a pleasant fact for me to cogitate while I'm being harassed like I was for the last month of the 1995 football season by Kansas City Chiefs fans who wanted my tail and ears for the crime of daring to tell the truth about their not great team.

But from the moment the Chiefs were upset in the playoffs by the Indianapolis Colts in a close game, I never got another call from Kansas City about anything. It's been months. The next time the Chiefs or Royals go anywhere, you can bet somebody in Kansas City will have learned a lesson on how not to look like a **goober.**

Any other small time–minded fans who might lose their minds and dignity to their team's temporary success might want to think over the following story. A couple years ago, an NFL wide receiver caught a ball for a touchdown, then danced and juked in the end zone. The referee watched this unasked-for revue for a moment, then went to reclaim the football in the end zone and said, "Act like you've been here before, son."

Get it? These cities all learned the ultimate Fabulous Sports Babe maxim that is guaranteed to provide for a long life: **"The Babe rules, and don't fuck with me."**

Class? All together now. Kansas City, Columbus, Seattle, and any other pinpoint on the map:

"The Babe rules, and don't fuck with her."

And these precepts are also aimed at Mormons, whom I respect a great deal. Still, I don't think it was necessary for my Salt Lake City affiliate to pull me off the air over a remark I made to somebody from Utah who'd called with a question about the Jazz-Rockets playoff game. "I don't know," I said innocently enough, "why don't you go call one of your wives?"

Ah, the fire and brimstone that fell for that one. The program director for the station that unplugged me told reporters that I "had a tendency to be **anti-Utah, anti—Western Athletic Conference, and anti-Jazz."**

Take a hike, you feebleminded, weak-charactered yes-man! You can bet that if there wasn't a feud between me and Utah before, there was certainly going to be one now. ESPN threatened to sue the radio station, and we were back on the air the next day. And now the station has new owners who carry the Babe in seven other markets. They love me. Get over it.

This mania can take over any city at any time. Everyone in Orlando, for example, thinks the Magic is the greatest basketball team ever.

Wrong. And I think I'm absolutely within my rights to point out to these yo-yos that the wrath of God will be brought down upon the Orlando Magic again, just as it was when Houston swept them four straight in the 1995 finals. I think it's my duty as a Pulitzer Prize–winning journalist and prognosticator to tell these Florida jugheads that *Michael Jordan and the Western Conference of the NBA exist to crush them.* The latest and best proof of the Bulls' dominance over the Orlando pretenders came when they blew the Magic away in four straight games in the 1996 semi-finals.

Me with Orlando coach Brian Hill. Hey, Brian, tell your team and your town to get a life! (And how are you going to play without the Shaq now, anyway?)

And then, when I impart the truth, these fanatics get angry, call me names, put me down as a cynic unwilling to believe in their sainted team. Go to hell, I say. I can't help it if nowadays fans in every city feel they have this undeniable **God-given right** to claim that they're number one in something. It doesn't matter if they live in Orlando, Kansas City, or Chicago, these Bubbas just have to feel that in one itty-bitty teeny-weeny part of their lives they are the best at something. It's enough for them if their championship is in the field of sitting on the couch watching what they have duped themselves into thinking is the greatest team in the solar system. *Their* team.

Poor chumps. Again, for callers past and future, please remember this simple commandment: **"The Babe rules, and don't fuck with me."** MEMORIZE IT. REMEMBER IT. LIVE BY IT. Someday, if you ever work up the courage to actually call "The Fabulous Sports Babe Show," it could save your life.

Five

The Babe's Baby II

Behind the Scenes at "The Fabulous Sports Babe Show" (Guests and Other Strangers)

We're not going to record this, right? You just want me to say my name and add a nice memory of Babe? OK.

This is Dan Patrick of ESPN. Don't record this, because it's just something that happened, and I don't want it out on the airwaves. Anyway, it was Cindy Crawford, Elle McPherson, me, and the Babe, and we were into our own little extreme games, if you know what I mean.

Well, the Babe is on a unicycle. . . . What, you want me to stop? Okay, I'll try it again some other time . . .

—Dan Patrick, ESPN Sportscenter anchor, in prerecorded message aired on the Fabulous Sports Babe's first anniversary show, July 4, 1995

A lot of the success of our show has to do with more than just knowing which people and cities to goof around with. Our guest list is the best in the business, and Babe-aholics know that every single day we'll have on major sports figures describing what happened last night at the all-important game or union meeting. I'm simply not interested in having as a guest some ***drooling old geezer*** who played for the 1918 St. Louis Browns.

A major reason we get the toughest, most sought-after guests on a second's notice is that with the Babe, they know they will find an intelligent ear and mouth. These qualities, to be sure, are absent among 99 percent of the sports radio talk show hosts now polluting the airwaves with their noxious fulminations.

The other reason the Fabulous Sports Babe is able to get the guests you **Babe-aholics** pine for is **Steve Barenfeld,** my show's producer and genius guest booker. Steve, trained as a bulldog sports reporter on a New York tabloid, plays his booker's telephone like Liberace tickled the ivories. Because Steve was trained as a tabloid sports guy, he's willing to be quite a nudge in getting what and who he wants. Steve will call and call and call a would-be guest, and since he knows a lot of people in the sports business he can usually get through.

Once Steve has got the sucker on the phone, he won't let up until he's gotten the person to come on the show. BOOKING GUESTS IS STEVE'S RELIGIOUS MISSION IN LIFE, his heavenly reward coming when he is finally able to get impossible-to-book guests on "The Fabulous Sports Babe Show."

Stevie, after we threw him in the dryer!

When a guest Steve has roped in is on the phone or sitting next to me in the studio, the duty shifts to me to get the sonuvabitch to both talk and be interesting. Here my doctorate in psychiatry from the Sorbonne comes in quite handy.

In general, baseball players are the hardest athletes to interview. For years, baseball players have been notorious for blowing off interviews they'd promised to reporters. In basketball and football, 99 percent of the players will give you what you want if you just wait long enough in the locker room after a game. But baseball players don't care—**some truly believe they are goddamn princes.**

This was so even back when I was a radio rat dragging my tape recorder through the sludge in order to get a usable comment or two to slap on the airwaves. I'd try and do my job, hanging out at the batting cage with the ballplayers trying to get them to talk. But the baseball players wouldn't even look at you, never mind engage you in conversation.

Hockey players are the best athletes to go to for comments and even politeness. Most hockey players remain moored to planet Earth because on some basic level they still don't understand why people are paying them to play hockey. Hockey players think it's the best thing in the world that they can play this game and then somebody hands them a check on Friday. They feel lucky to be playing the game, and as long as they have that mentality you can bet that they will be more than OK to deal with.

Few people in other professional sports feel this way. Baseball players were the first to approach their game as merely a business, and were quickly followed by football and basketball players. Even hockey players, I imagine, will someday soon begin acting like the *prima donna* **assholes** who predominate in other sports.

Hockey players have also been incredibly loyal to me and my show over the years. During the hockey lockout last year, all the hockey players used "The Fabulous Sports Babe Show" as their information central. Many players were calling me off the air to give me information about what was really going down that day with the lockout, and I was pleased to offer my show as a forum to end the deadlock.

It worked. Players and management used us as a daily sounding board to gauge the intent of the other side. They argued with each other with me serving as referee, and like Solomon I told them to cut the baby in half. **And the Babe now takes full credit for solving the hockey lockout.** My show is the court of opinion, and my listeners and I made sure that the dispute was solved before the game, and our collective lives, were ruined forever.

Babe's Best Bets

I predict the **NHL** players will change their minds and refuse to start the season when they realize the fine print in the contract mandates that they must buy their own sticks, skates, and uniforms, pay their own plane fare, and work as Zamboni drivers between periods.

And I predict Barry Switzer will protest the Cowboys' playoff loss to San Francisco, saying the field was too muddy, the officials made too many mistakes, the timekeeper was unfair, the 49er players were too rough, he needed more time to prepare for the game, Jerry Jones bothered him too much . . .

Like hockey players, basketball players are normally pretty OK to talk to. Usually it's quiet in the locker room after a game, and you only have to deal with a dozen players on one team. For some reason, basketball players generally realize that it's their job to talk to reporters, and most go about it methodically.

It's weird, but I've never met a basketball player who was real outgoing, gregarious, and wild. They're usually very quiet people, which might stem, I think, from the fact that they have been **physical freaks** their entire lives. At thirteen years old, they were all 6'4" tall and gangly. The self-consciousness that comes with that height never really goes away for a lot of them.

Football players can be very tough to interview, especially after they've just lost a game. Because they have fewer games than other professional sports, their highs and lows are much more distinct. One loss to a football player can be devastating, while a player on the New York Knicks might casually say, "We lost that game because we didn't get pressure up-court." One loss to a basketball player just doesn't make that big a difference.

You would think that baseball players would be the mellowest of the jock lot. With 162 games to play, they can quite literally come back tomorrow after a loss and win. Still, these guys are the hardest to pin down for reasons nobody understands. While they were all growing up, baseball was still the **national pastime**—and they were treated like princes headed to the throne. I guess most of these ballplayers never got over that feeling that they were better then the rest of us.

The biggest dicks in any sport are usually the nobodies. You can usually count on the fact that the player being the biggest asshole is the second-string quarterback who barely made the team this year but now thinks he's Joe Montana. These are the fuckers who haven't even earned their kiss-my-ass attitude.

Other players simply can't integrate it into their tiny worldview that a woman could actually be doing my job, and doing it well. The most disgusting example of this kind of idiot behavior came in 1994, when I was going to interview Gary Plummer of the **San Francisco 49ers** at practice. Plummer, on the phone, simply refused to cooperate. He out-and-out didn't believe that a woman could be doing this show. He was entirely convinced that he was being set up in some sort of elaborate practical joke.

In his own sexist reality, he just couldn't believe that a woman could know anything about football. Finally, I threw down my headphones and said that I didn't need to do this interview with this numbnut. "I've put up with this shit for years," I told my producer, "and I didn't need to fuck with it today."

But no matter what team or sport a reporter covers, he or she knows there are players who you can go to for good quotes and stories all the time. Some of these quotables are looking ahead in their lifetimes to when they're through playing sports and might want to get into the media themselves. Others are simply good guys. Either way, they are the sports reporter's salvation.

Many athletes are reluctant to talk, of course, because *some sports reporters are such stone* **assholes.** I've observed so many so-called professional reporters ask the stupidest, most asinine questions of athletes that I sometimes wonder if idiocy is a job requirement to be hired on in the sports department of some newspapers and television stations.

Needless to say, the reporting is not getting any better. Back in Babe Ruth's day, the sporting press was perceived by teams as an extension of their club's public relations department. The last several decades have seen an increase in the amount of investigative reporting done by these former shills, the sports journalists.

Some sports reporters aren't afraid to call up some player's DYING GRANDMOTHER to get an inflammatory quote, and the players are getting ever more pissed. Almost all sports reporting has now gone the tabloid route, and in some ways I don't think that's bad. THE *NATIONAL ENQUIRER*, REMEMBER, WAS RIGHT ABOUT EVERY SINGLE THING INVOLVING O. J. SIMPSON, **that lying, murdering bastard.**

Babe's Best Bets

The Babe predicts O. J. Simpson will place an unsolicited call to the Babe and reveal his deepest, darkest secret . . . that he's always dreamed of being the Sportsboy.

Within the fraternity of **JOCK-SNIFFING REPORTERS** there is a pecking order. The bottom rung is occupied by radio reporters, who are considered dog shit by television and print sports journalists. Television guys, meantime, are looked down upon by the newspaper people. It's a bullshit way of looking at the media world, but it remains deeply ingrained in many of the sports press boxes.

I still remember back in the 1980s when Tampa Bay Buccaneers coach Ray Perkins had been fired. Perkins, the dick, had called a press conference but decreed that only print reporters could attend. I was insane with rage. You can't call a press conference and then decide who in the press can come. Still, they locked me out of the Buccaneers pressroom, making it necessary for me to bang and kick the door and start screaming that I was going to call the police because my constitutional rights as an accredited member of the media were being violated. **HOO-WAH!**

I was going to break a window, a fact everyone in that room knew. Meanwhile, all the television guys with no balls stood outside with me as I was shrieking obscenities and kicking down the door. Fuck it, I didn't care. I never shied away from a fight in my life. And finally, I was admitted to that hallowed hall to hear the secret stop-the-presses explanations of why Coach Ray Perkins had gotten canned.

Now it's no secret that many athletes despise the reporters who cover them. But that doesn't really matter to me, because I have the use of **STEVE BARENFELD,** the genius guest booker on "The Fabulous Sports Babe Show," to get them all.

An apple a day keeps the Babe at bay!!!

Steve is truly a marvel at his job. To put it simply, **Steve was born to book.** And God loves Steve for his attitude that good guests are prized quarry meant to be brought down and strapped to the roof of his car like a hunted deer. But goddamnit if Steve's style of hunting down guests doesn't work. More than anyone, he is responsible for most of my favorite all-time interviews on the show.

Somehow, he even got **Faye Vincent,** the ex-commissioner of baseball, who'd refused to talk to any reporters since he'd been fired by the owners. Well, of course, Faye Vincent talked on-air with the Fabulous Sports Babe for a fascinating hour. But that would never have happened if Stevie hadn't warmed him up with four months of pleading phone calls promising that Vincent could have his say in the most righteous forum in the Western world.

This is not to say "The Fabulous Sports Babe Show" is meant to be "Meet the Press." Screwing around with news and newsmakers is part of our public service, and **we take it SERIOUSLY.**

One of my favorite stunts happened in the spring of 1995 when the baseball players were on strike and the owners were looking for replacements to put on the field. The Colorado Rockies even went so far as to put an ad in *USA Today* saying they were seeking players to play scab ball. Listed there in the newspaper was a phone number. Of course, our crack team of researchers were tipped off to the ad. We quickly decided to have a little fun at the expense of these idiots who thought they could field a team through the want ads.

So I called up the number on the air and announced that my name was *Madame Rolonda* and that I was representing two fine prospects from the Dominican Republic who would like to play for the Rockies. Denis the Sportsboy then got on the telephone and said in a fractured accent, "MY NAME IS JIMINY MARTIGUEZ. I'M AMPHIBIOUS—I CAN THROW WITH EITHER HAND."

Lenny the Phone Freak then got on the phone and said, **"I keeck a touchdown!"** Ah, good old-fashioned phone fun. But this goof also served to reinforce the absurdity of the replacement player solution.

Some of the most fun we have is when we actually get out of the ESPN studio in **Petticoat Junction** and take the show on the

Top Ten Slogans for the 1995 Baseball Season

10. Replacement fever: It's like typhoid fever, but not fatal!

9. Same game, more guys named Ed.

8. The only sport with a World Series every couple of years!

7. Bring the kids. Their tickets are only $5 more!

6. Buy me some peanuts and Cracker Jacks, they were delivered by the left fielder!

5. It can't be worse than watching the O. J. Simpson trial!

4. Hey, it's not like we're bringing in Roseanne to sing the national anthem!

3. Replacement baseball: Yeah, it sucks, but what are you gonna do?

2. Hey, just three short months to NFL training camps!

1. Please, please, please, please, please come see a game!

road in front of real live fans. One trip was to Detroit, which was one of the first cities to support the Fabulous Sports Babe when she arrived at ESPN.

Back then at the beginning, the **Global Babe Network** consisted of only twenty-eight stations, a number that would soon increase eightfold. But we always got a tremendous response from Detroit, getting a ton of calls from the Motor City. Indeed, so many early callers to the show were from Detroit that we had to start weeding them out so it didn't sound like "The Fabulous Sports Babe Show" was a local vehicle for the sports teams of the city.

Anyway, after a year and a half on the air, we finally went to broadcast from this huge sports bar in Detroit. The place was completely packed, and fans were lined up outside around the block and six people deep. People came up to touch the hem of my garment as if I were the DALAI LAMA. All in all, it was a very moving scene.

The event also served to remind me not to get a big head. I've done live broadcasts where there were twenty people in the room, and I'll never forget that feeling. Those memories keep me humble, and serve to guarantee that I will never turn into **Zsa Zsa Gabor,** no matter my fame or power.

It was fun to be able to interact with fans again. One of the hardest things about working for ESPN is that we're stranded out in the **Petticoat Junction boonies** without any real people to interact with. When I was working in Tampa or Seattle, I could walk into any sports bar and run into folks who'd want to talk about last night's game or today's show. They'd ask for my autograph, bitch about some lousy trade the Sonics made, and a good time would be had by all.

I have none of that in Petticoat Junction. I walk out the door and there's no one there. No one knows who I am or where I live, because my show is no longer a locally based program where you're out there in the community every day.

Now, if I go see a Hartford Whalers game—the closest major league contests to Petticoat Junction—barely anybody there is aware that the Fabulous Sports Babe is in their presence. I actually prefer it, because I can finally have some peace, but if it weren't for the road, I might sometimes actually forget that I am the Fabulous Sports Babe.

It is in the office, however, where the Fabulous Sports Babe truly rules. I'm not sure how women bosses are supposed to behave, because I've never had one. Radio is a **testosterone-fueled business,** and I've never dealt with a woman working as my boss.

My own management style is to rant and rave, shoot from the hip, and not pull any punches with the people who work for me. I'm not insane in the office, but I like things done just so. Sometimes I will say "You fucked up" to someone who works for me instead of using one of the nice words you're supposed to use when you're the boss. This does not make me a war criminal.

ESPN Radio's Chuck Wilson. I love him!! Everything about him is completely opposite of me, yet I respect him and his observations more than most!!

I don't use phrases like "WE NEED MORE SYNERGY AMONGST OUR COMRADES IN THE WORK GROUP" or *"We need to address these issues and challenges as a team."* Rather, I'd prefer to just say, **"You BASTARD, you SCREWED UP. Now how are you going to fix it in the seconds before I FIRE YOU?"** This is what I call true leadership.

So I yell at my charges all day long; nothing gets people going like shouting into the newsroom, "You bastards, I hate you!" My staff knows I'm kidding—and they also know I'm serious. When I use a certain tone of voice, my underlings also know that I'm goddamn mad and that they better drop everything and go make mama happy. At the same time that I'm playing Kathy Bates in *Misery*, however, I'm also holding on tight to my credo that if I'm not having a good time at work then I won't be back. That's why I make the working atmosphere at "The Fabulous Sports Babe Show" similar to that found on the first day of kindergarten. OK, to be honest, let's call working on my show **half kindergarten, half gulag. HOO-WAH!**

But even though I torture my staff, how many people at their jobs are allowed to dance around all day and snap their fingers? That's what they do on my staff, because this is showbiz, and we're just putting on a show.

Denis the Sportsboy endures the bulk of my wrath, just

So many assholes. So many phone lines.

because he deserves it. Being bullied and battered by me during the day, then chained to the radiator in my trailer by night, might not seem like a dream job. But as Denis the Sportsboy knows, there are a million people waiting in line for his job. Sportsboy knows this, and this knowledge keeps him somewhat in line. Still, I feel the need to reinforce in him the knowledge that he is at all times only one heartbeat away from Palookaville. Tough love, I tell Sportsboy as I debase him and make him eat dog food, is the best love of all.

Denis, needless to say, was not enthusiastic when I made an offhand comment on the show during the spring of 1995 about how I was now taking applications for the soon-to-be-vacated Sportsboy position.

The Fabulous Sports Babe Sportsboy Application

TOP TEN REASONS I SHOULD BE HIRED AS YOUR SPORTSBOY

10. I had a brief tenure as an Ohio State football player, but was fired by the fans!

9. The only twenty-three-year-old African-American male who thinks O. J. Simpson is guilty!!

8. Played as a scab baseball player, but quit after being placed lower on the depth chart than Larry Bud Melman!

7. Once played a pickup basketball game with Michael Jackson, Lisa Marie Presley, and the monkey!!

6. I eat and throw octopi for breakfast!

5. If asked where a team is now, I will not tell you what the road trip will be like to Pittsburgh! (Ahh . . . uhuh uhuh Eric Turner.)

4. Will not make a complete fool of myself hosting and singing on "Saturday Night Live" like Deion Sanders!

3. Positively sure that I could make two out of four free throws during the NBA finals with both eyes closed!

2. Will be legally changing my name to "Jeff Gillooly."

1. The number one reason I should be hired as the Fabulous Sports Babe Sportsboy is, I will do anything to get out of the plumber's butt of America, Columbus, Ohio.

"This guy is so terrible," I complained to my listeners, "and I just can't take it anymore. I need a new Sportsboy." I told my listeners that I'd had a Sportsboy with me for ten years, and that the beautiful part of my show is that I can fire anybody because their on-air characters all belong to me—they are all instantly replaceable.

I don't need a cast of thousands, I explained to my audience, because Sportsboy is a wonderful whipping boy who symbolizes every put-upon male on the planet. Well, within seconds of my faux announcement that I was looking for a new Sportsboy, people began sending us résumés from every state in the country.

These idiots thought we were serious! They believed in their idiot heads that I was replacing Sportsboy, and they seriously wanted to apply for the position!

I thought this was just great. I couldn't help but laugh at all these **assholes FedExing me real** résumés. And they were assholes. Anybody who sends me a real résumé can't possibly understand my show. If listeners take me at face value, they simply aren't listening to my message as empress of the theater of the mind.

And yet there were times when I was tempted to make true my threats to Sportsboy's livelihood. He once lost our airplane tickets from Detroit back to Petticoat Junction, a feat even now I have trouble fathoming. "What do you mean?" I shrieked. "Fucking guy loses our tickets! When we get back I am truly going to be taking applications!" Sportsboy whimpered. Lucky for him we managed to get on a plane.

Against my better judgment, I've begun cutting Sportsboy some more slack. I let him actually leave the trailer once in a while, and I bought him his own doghouse that sits near the satellite dish. If you watch the opening cartoon sequence on the ESPN2 version of my show, you can marvel at the workmanship that went into Sportsboy's new domicile.

The campaign for a new Sportsboy went on and off for a year, and I'm sure we'll do it again. I like to beat the shit out of a joke until it's hammered deep into the ground. Then we'll let the bit rest for a couple of months before bringing it back.

Date: 12/8/95

To: 1(800)592-3776

Attn: The Sports Babe

I sent this to you a couple of days ago and never heard from you. Since I've never gotten anything I wanted without being a pest, here we go again!

APPLICATION FOR THE SPORTSBOY
DOUGLAS ARMSTRONG

I played four years of high school football.

I will insist that Craig James give Southwest Hooterville City Junior Barber College for the Deaf and Blind the **RESPECT** they deserve.

My bowling average is almost as high as my golf average.

I used to live in Portland and I know why it's called the PLUMBER'S BUTT.

I've had my rabies shot.

Before I met the Babe and learned the error of my ways, I was commissioner of my fantasy synchronized swimming league.

For a fat bald man, I don't sweat much.

I'm just getting back now to playing selections from the **Royal Babe Orchestra** after beating that routine to death and beyond. I was getting temporarily bored with my symphony, but when listeners started making requests for the Babe's orchestra again, I knew it was safe to bring back the goods.

But "The Fabulous Sports Babe Show" is not solely about shtick and other assorted bullshit. Everyone on my **corrupt and bedraggled staff** takes pride in the fact that we truly want to talk about the issues. This is what makes us different from your average talk radio sports show featuring idiot men jerking off while they wonder and talk about how this one guy can be batting .320 while that other bastard is only batting .220. Who, I wonder, really cares?

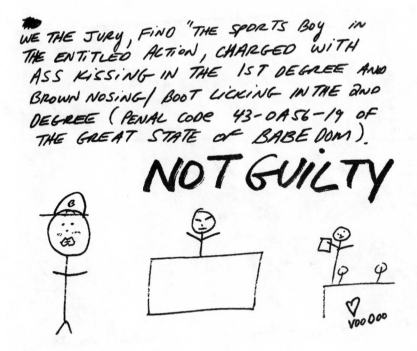

We're not afraid to go out on a limb on "The Fabulous Sports Babe Show" and let the radio studios get a little mussed and humid with some real hard talk. Some of our shining moments, of course, came during those blackest of times for sports fans. The hockey and baseball strikes sucked majorly, but for the Babe they provided the mother lode of material.

One of our most intense shows during the baseball strike involved Bob Scanlon, a pitcher for the Milwaukee Brewers who was one of our frequent guests reporting on the labor situation. Anyway, we once induced Bob to come on the show with one of the replacement players who'd been signed to take the striking players' places.

The so-called scab player was a new Kansas City Royal named Scott Anderson. For an hour, Anderson and Scanlon went after each other like angry jackals. It was incredible radio as these guys alternated between slamming each other, taking phone calls, and trying to convince each other of the righteousness of their causes.

What was cool was that when the hour was over and the bash-

Heckyl and Jeckyl, decorators to the Babe.
They're the ones who make the Airstream look fabulous.

ing was done, both really seemed to have grown in respect in the eyes of the other. **I am the United fucking Nations!**

Things got a tad more surreal during the strike when we put on another debate featuring a striking ballplayer and a replacement. This time we got brothers to hatchet each other. Mike Aldretti of the Oakland A's represented the real Major Leaguers in this forum, while the replacement players were spoken for by Rich Aldretti, momentarily employed by the Milwaukee Brewers.

It was interesting to hear Mike, who'd had a nice career already in the Majors, try and talk his brother out of crossing the picket line. Rich, meantime, simply wanted to make the point that he was just trying to make a living. Not as talented as his brother, Rich pointed out, this was probably his only chance to ever wear a Major League uniform.

Good shit. As was the shit that came over the air that day during the strike when my usually idiot staff convinced me to have

Pete Rose on the program. I've already stated my opinion on Pete Rose: **The bastard knows he bet on baseball, we know he bet on baseball, so why doesn't he just confess and throw himself on the mercy of the court of public opinion?**

But OK, I finally consented, Pete Rose can come on the show. It's not like I'm sucking up to him, I said, or lobbying that his

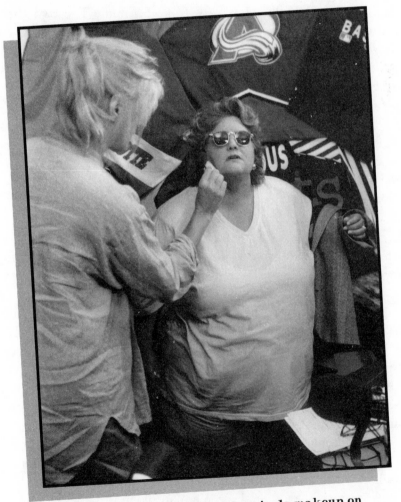

Linda the makeup queen. I refuse to do makeup on Babe TV—it just negates the point!—so she only helps out when I'm in magazines and newspapers.

kisser should be enshrined on a plaque in Cooperstown. So the day comes and we're on the radio with Pete Rose, talking about this, that, and the strike, when a call comes in from a guy identifying himself as "Mike from Dayton." Mike has a question for Pete Rose.

"Who is the best player you ever saw or played with?" ASKED THE CALLER.

"**Mike Schmidt**," Pete Rose said **without** hesitation.

Good guess, because **"Mike from DAYTON"** was none other than Pete's old Philly teammate Mike Schmidt. The two then spent the next twenty minutes reminiscing about the game as they remember it. It was amazing to be reminded in the middle of the strike of what baseball used to be about. Needless to say this isn't what it's about anymore, a fact that blows so mightily I can't say it too loud or long.

The beginning of the strike gave us some good squishy radio as well. I still remember having Bill Giles of the Philadelphia Phillies on the program. Man, how my body shook as Giles came out with the previously unreported fact that there indeed would be no World Series that year. I couldn't believe it when Giles made his little announcement. Say it ain't so, Bill.

But instead I croaked out, *"Bill, what would your late father think if he heard the World Series had been canceled?"* His father, of course, was the late, great Warren Giles, one-time president and grand old man of the National League.

"Right now my father is rolling in his grave," is all Bill said sadly. They were the deepest words I heard all week.

Some of the most interesting stories of the strike, however, came from people only tangentially connected to the game. We heard at one point from Howard Hart, a guy who'd been selling hot dogs at Baltimore Orioles games for **thirty years**. Now, in the middle of the strike, he was forced to drive down to the Carolina League in order to peddle his frankfurters. Howard provided a real look at how the baseball strike affected more than just millionaire ballplayers and billionaire owners. There's nothing like the keen insight of a good weenie man when it comes to understanding labor relations.

George Steinbrenner, another of Babe's devoted legion, was a frequent guest during the strike. He rewarded us for providing him this pulpit later that year when the Yankees played the Seattle Mariners in the playoffs. George graciously offered Sportsboy and me tickets to the playoff opener in his private box, and we enjoyed exchanging salutations with fellow revelers like SPIKE LEE and **REGGIE JACKSON.**

I felt a little bad that Sportsboy and I spent all of our days in New York playing, partying, and interviewing my beloved Mariners. The Yankees got almost no coverage on my scope. Yet I rationalized that even though sitting in George Steinbrenner's seats were nice, I simply had to hang with my Seattle homeboys. **HOO-WAH!**

But it is important to point out that I am never a homer, except for my Boston teams. **Though I love the Seattle Mariners, I relish each time I get to skewer that pompous fuck of a town that I call Hooterville.**

I proved that not long ago when we had Jane Hague of the Seattle City Council on the show to discuss the Seattle Seahawks. The team had threatened at that point to leave Seattle because the Kingdome was vulnerable to earthquakes. So I ask her about it, and in typical Seattle fashion she says, "WE HAVE GUARANTEED 100 PERCENT THAT THE KINGDOME WILL BE **seismically** CORRECT."

Seismically correct? Excuse me? Everything that is wrong with that town is in that statement, as is every reason I wanted to leave that lousy town. Seismically correct?

Sometimes it isn't our guests who are berated in their seats, but my devoted staff of far-flung correspondents. One of my best, of course, is that strange human being Mel Kiper. Mel bills himself as the NFL draft expert, and that he surely is. The draft is truly his life, and up until a short time ago he lived in the basement of his father's town house in Baltimore. There, Mel did nothing else but study rosters and player placements.

We like Mel and all our experts to have no life. That way, we know that our experts have taken the time to be the absolute smartest in the world. Sadly, the Colts general manager Bill Tobin didn't realize Mel's godlike powers a couple of drafts ago.

"You better draft a quarterback," Mel advised him. Tobin listened, then proceeded to go off on our beloved draft expert on the

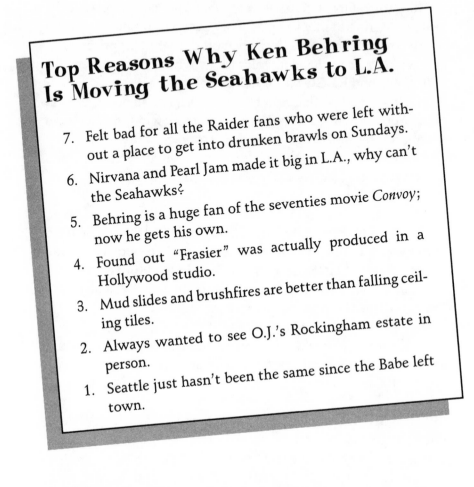

Top Reasons Why Ken Behring Is Moving the Seahawks to L.A.

7. Felt bad for all the Raider fans who were left without a place to get into drunken brawls on Sundays.

6. Nirvana and Pearl Jam made it big in L.A., why can't the Seahawks?

5. Behring is a huge fan of the seventies movie *Convoy*; now he gets his own.

4. Found out "Frasier" was actually produced in a Hollywood studio.

3. Mud slides and brushfires are better than falling ceiling tiles.

2. Always wanted to see O.J.'s Rockingham estate in person.

1. Seattle just hasn't been the same since the Babe left town.

air. He began by telling Mel what an idiot he was, then began hitting below the belt.

"Who the HELL are you?" the general manager demanded of Mel. "When is the last time you wore a jock?" He got very nasty, but of course, Mel was right. Tobin's team did need a quarterback, and they idiotically didn't draft one. Of course, Tobin had to go out and pick up veteran quarterback Jim Harbaugh the next year. Good work, Mel! Another great story about Mel took place on 1996 NFL Draft Day, when Mel and Joe Theismann almost came to serious blows on the ESPN set when they fought about Nebraska running back Lawrence Phillips. People across the country were wagering on who would kick whose ass.

Sometimes, we're able at "The Fabulous Sports Babe Show" to expose the **EVIL UNDERBELLY** in athletics at a time when every other sports talk show on the planet seems to be discussing the merits of pizza versus grinders on Fantasy Football draft day. One of my on-air efforts I'm most proud about is the time we exposed to the country an anti-Semitic act aimed at Long Beach State basketball coach Seth Greenberg.

A year or two ago, Long Beach State had traveled to play a game against New Mexico State. When Coach Seth Greenberg walked into the visitors' locker room before the game, he flipped over the chalkboard in order to deliver a lecture. However, what he found written on the chalkboard was "Get out of town you Jew bastard."

There was a quite profound attempt to sweep this little incident under the rug. But the Babe wasn't about to let those bastards do it, and I kept harping on the issue on the air until it was made evident that this type of incident wouldn't be tolerated. I brought Coach Greenberg onto the show, and America heard.

Yes, we are unafraid to listen to the harshest truths, no matter what the cost. Twice during the baseball strike we even had on Labor Secretary Robert Reich to discuss the situation.

I love Mr. Reich because he is a die-hard Red Sox fan, but I made, I feel, a faux pas on the show in the way I referred to my distinguished guest, who is about 4'6". Twice I called him **"big guy"** on "The Fabulous Sports Babe Show," and now I understand that my passport has been revoked.

Sometimes we are not so lucky with heavy thinkers. We've had Tim Russert of "Meet the Press" on a couple times, and though I can't remember why, *I recall him to have been a prick.*

And sometimes we even break the news, not just spin it. When the NHL lockout was settled, Pittsburgh Penguin Larry Murphy was the one who called the Babe to break news of the breakthrough. SO WHERE IS OUR PULITZER FOR PUBLIC SERVICE REPORTING?

Nor were we given any awards after the hockey strike was over when we gave out the phone number of the famed octopus lady. For decades, hockey fans have thrown octopi on the ice after their team scores a goal in the playoffs. Now, with the number of the octopus lady, puck fans could call and get an octopus FedExed to them in time to throw said cephalopod on the ice at tomorrow night's game. Within limits, the public has a right to its own weirdness.

I will not, however, abide by bullshit coming from a politician. When the New Jersey Devils were in the Stanley Cup Finals, we had New Jersey Governor Christine Whitman on to discuss what the Devils meant to the state. I began by telling the governor, "Thanks for being on."

She came back with, "There is no other show I'd rather be a guest on."

What a fucking politician! I thought. **YOU NEVER EVEN HEARD OF MY SHOW! GET OUT!**

Other nonathletes fare much better. The comedian **Jackie Mason** was great, even though I introduced him not as a star of a one-man Broadway show but as the voice of the anteater on the Pink Panther cartoons. I can't quite recall what the deeper message of his rap was, but I do remember Jackie saying the salary cap should be renamed the "salary yarmulke."

Also among my two favorite nonathletes I ever had on the show were **Tommy Smothers** and **Bill Murray,** who talked to us at seven in the morning from the Pebble Beach golf course. Tommy was fun, and then he handed the microphone over to Bill, who I'm not sure even knew what my show was. Still, he talked, an honor that befits a man who I hear owns that tournament. He can do whatever he wants there, much to the horror of the old farts of golf—and the delight of fans who unfortunately need to look to the comedians to find any entertainment in the sport.

I know I'd rather watch Bill "Cinderella Story" Murray's golf movie *Caddyshack* for the millionth time than be forced to observe that **Aussie asshole Greg Norman** strolling down the fairway.

Six

A Portrait of the Artist as a Young Babe

Hi there, this is the Boomer, Chris Berman. My favorite Babe memory? Oh yeah, there was that one summer evening long ago when Babe and I went parking. The roof was down, the stars were out, we were pulled over to the side of the road. Then I woke up and yelled, "It ain't me, Babe, it ain't me you're looking for, Babe!" Happy anniversary, Hon. . . .
**—ESPN's Chris Berman,
on the Fabulous Sports Babe's
first anniversary show, July 4, 1995**

I believe it was Babe-raham Lincoln who was the first to point out that a house divided against itself cannot stand. Growing up in a forever moving household dominated by discouragement if not downright dysfunction, I understand. My parents didn't believe in what I was ever doing, and the end result was that I felt like I didn't really have a family at all.

Ever since I was a kid I've been a **sports fanatic.** I always liked playing and watching sports, but I came from a family that wasn't into athletics and never encouraged me at all. They always thought my interest in sports was weird. They just didn't care how much I enjoyed playing basketball and baseball; for my folks, sports were a bizarre departure from the preparations they thought I should be making toward becoming a human Barbie doll.

It wasn't just sports they were down on, though. Rather, I was the only child of parents who pooh-poohed my endeavors at all times, no matter what I did. My mother and stepfather were older, more traditional people who thought I should stop wasting my time with boys' games and start concentrating on more of the things that girls and women traditionally do.

To them, **a woman should be a secretary or home-**

maker, NOT A DOCTOR OR A LAWYER. As a girl, I couldn't dream of becoming a veterinarian, in their opinion, but rather a veterinarian's assistant. Naturally, none of that bullshit interested me.

My stepfather, the man of the house I knew growing up, was an officer in the air force. We were constantly moving as his postings shifted; I never lived anywhere for more then three years until I left home and went to college. That's why I don't now know a single soul from the myriad of academies I attended for grammar and high school. It's hard to bond with people as a teenager when, like me, you attend six different high schools.

Luckily, I was always happily adept at being alone. That's where my iron will comes from—the fact that as an only child constantly moving, I had to learn to amuse myself. I've always been a solitary person, and if I didn't learn to play by myself I would have ended up boring myself to death, **abso-Gillooly.**

My salvation always came in the form of electric boxes. From my first seconds of **BABE-CONSCIOUSNESS,** I was fascinated by television and radio. The television was my baby-sitter, while the radio was my dream machine. Luckily for me my family drove everywhere. So if my stepfather was transferred from Louisiana to California, we would take five days to drive. For most of the way we could pick up clear channel stations stretching all the way back to WHO in Des Moines. It was an entire universe controlled by six buttons on the car dashboard.

Even as a tiny girl I remember sitting in the back of my parents' car driving to some new state, concentrating only on the sounds coming out of the different buttons on the radio. My favorite radio performers from those long trips were the irreverent George Carlin and Richard Pryor, who could play with words and ideas like nobody I'd heard before. God, I loved them.

There was something magical about the radio that I plugged in to from the first moments my ear could make out words. I can still remember listening as a very little girl in Louisiana to an NBC Radio piece about how Christmas was celebrated across the world. I felt transported, and never forgot that piece.

I suppose the fact that I never really lived anywhere accounts for how it doesn't bother me now to just pick up from a city and move somewhere else. Friends were shocked that I could just split from Florida for Seattle like I did, but it didn't strike me as anything traumatic at all. My whole life, it seemed, had been spent in the back of my parents' car as we crisscrossed the country to another of his bases. In some ways, this deep-down living and breathing with the radio was the best education I ever had.

It was from the radio that I first learned of the majesty of black music. I was seven and temporarily living in Montgomery, Alabama, when I got turned on to Etta James, Joe Williams, and Frogman Henry. Even at seven I remember saying out loud, **"THIS FUCKING MUSIC IS GREAT!" HOO-WAH!**

So I listened, and listened some more, to any music or announcer who could make me say, *"What up wit' dat?"* The radio was my friend, because I didn't have anybody else. As I sat in the backseat alone with the dog, going from one end of the country to another, the radio was the one constant in my life. This was when I realized how radio truly was the **theater of the mind.** I just loved the sound of the action, the announcers, even the silence.

One of my earliest memories is taking the radio into my Catholic school's bathroom during the World Series because I wanted to hear every pitch of the game. *The nuns were absolutely positive I was smoking cigarettes in there.* But it was only the radio keeping me there, the only reality I cared about. True, some of those places radio took me weren't realities where I wanted to go (Who wants to hear their team die in the World Series?), but the radio was a force, I knew, and I wanted to be part of its power.

The radio, I realized very early in life, was also a weird kind of glue that could bond communities to themselves. The importance of this antiquated notion hit me once again only months before I went on the air with ESPN in July 1994.

That spring, I drove with ESPN Radio's Mark Mason up near Lake George for a meeting of the ABC sales staff. During a break from the festivities, I took the rental car out for a ride around the resort and tuned in the one radio station in the whole region.

I couldn't believe what I was hearing. As the minutes went on, the announcer talked about how someone in town had lost their

dog, and read some obituary notices. He then followed up these scintillating tidbits with school
lunch and senior citizens menus for the day. There
was a garage sale over on Main Street, I learned, and
a kitten was available for free somewhere else.

I was amazed by the power this little station with
its small-town announcements had over me. I immediately drove back to the resort and ordered Mark
Mason to take a drive to nowhere with the radio
on. "You have to hear this," I told him, shoving him
into the car like he was a suspect on "Cops."

I commandeered him because this little dinky station was the
embodiment of all that radio was supposed to be. **RADIO, I
REMEMBERED, WAS NOT ABOUT THE FABULOUS
SPORTS BABE SHOW REACHING ZILLIONS. RATHER,
IT'S ABOUT COMMUNITY SERVICE.** Mark wasn't surprised by my passion, because he already knew that I'm one of the
few people left on the planet who still actually believes in the public service aspect of radio broadcasting.

**Mark Mason—I gave him an
earful about the community
of radio!**

As we listened, I told Mark that
I'd forgotten stations still do this—
tell whose dog was missing, whose
friend was dead, and what day
Sloppy Joes would be served over
at the community center. This
was radio serving as town crier,
exactly what AM stations are supposed to be. The radio could and
should serve as an extended family to entire communities.

Since the beginning of my life,
radio has actually served as my
entire family. I don't really have
any interaction with my family
anymore, but I don't say this as if
I've suffered some grievous loss. I
just never cared that I didn't
have a close relationship with

my folks. To be honest, I feel as if everything I've accomplished in life has been in spite of my family's lack of support.

I think you reach a point in life where it just doesn't matter anymore if people have any clue as to what you're doing or what you're about. At some point you need to move on.

A long time ago I started removing people from my life who weren't adding positive energy. After a while you just say, "Who needs it?" and wave good-bye to those who drag you down.

So, the day I turned eighteen, I put my ass on an airplane and never once went back to their house. I don't talk much about the past or revel in tales of the good old days, because it just wasn't very good. Radio, and the friends I made in radio, would be my new family, the place I could always run to if things didn't work out. The oldest friend I have is somebody I've known since I was nineteen—and that's when my life actually began.

Me and my friend Tommy in 1979—he had a lot more hair then and I'm even better looking now!

I spent much of the seventies kicking around pieces of the country figuring out how to dip my ass in the turbulent waters of radio. I checked into colleges in Boston, checked out, and tried the campus scene in Florida. Deep in the back of my mind I knew I

My friend Allen modeling Babe gear.

wanted to do sports radio, but since no one in the country back then was going to hire a woman to do sports, I was smart enough to just enjoy life.

Even though no one would hire me to do what I wanted on the radio, I never thought I couldn't do sports radio just because I was a woman. Once I was on the path, I was like a **militant Muslim on jihad.** I always knew I would make it, triumphing over the Great Satan of sexism and idiocy to speak my mind on athletics and the world over the radio. It was just a matter of time, guts, and paying dues.

I was already pretty smart about the radio business, and knew there were many other obstacles to my success other than the fact that I bore ovaries. For one, I always knew there was a percentage of this business that was sleazy, a portion of the industry run by the dirtiest scumbags on the show business planet.

Why? Well, for a very long time, owning a radio station has been a license to print money. Typically, a communications company would buy a station, fire everybody who worked there, cut the budget to the bone, then resell the place for a quick, tidy profit. Many companies have made very nice fortunes by flipping stations and making a quick buck by screwing over everyone who works there. **Bastards!**

I can't tell you how many times I've been fired in the midst of corporate bullshit. I can't tell you because I can't remember—after a while you tend to lose count of how many times you've been dicked over by BEAN COUNTERS and **corporate bloodsuckers**.

One of my early jobs was as a talk show host on a Florida station. Things went nicely for a couple of years, and then one day, at four in the afternoon, bingo. We were suddenly an all-business radio station, and forty people were out of a job. **HOO·WAH!**

Another time I was playing rock and roll records at a fabulous station out east when suddenly the place was sold and at midnight they began playing religious music. Another one of the best stations I'd ever been on blew up at exactly twelve A.M. when a van drove up

My best friend Boodgie and her girls.

filled with people carrying their new music, commercial carts, and call letters literally in their hands. GOOD MORNING, VIETNAM, indeed.

It's a mean business, I learned early on, but big deal. You know how this game is played when you're breaking in or you're an idiot. So I paid attention, learned how to read a room, and paid more dues than a lifelong member of the Shriners.

I didn't really have any idols on the radio as I was coming up. A lot of guys in the sports radio business will say they patterned themselves after **Bob Costas, Curt Gowdy, Mel Allen,** or whoever happened to broadcast in their hometown when they were growing up. I didn't have any idols in the true sense of the word, because I didn't want to do play-by-play sports announcing.

Rather, I wanted to do sports talk radio, a format that began to fascinate me in Boston in the 1970s. If I was a disciple of anyone, it was **EDDIE ANDELMAN,** who had a show every Sunday on WHDH from seven in the evening until midnight.

Eddie was so irreverent it was unbelievable—his show was completely revolutionary for its time. If the germ and attitude of the Fabulous Sports Babe began anywhere, it was with the great Eddie. **(Eddie—back off.)** Boston also has the incomparable Bob Lobel at WBZ. His on-air attitude is just as scabrous and smart-alecky, and he too ranks as one of my top influences.

So I knew in the back of my mind that someday I would like to do sports talk radio. But in the very beginning of my career, all I truly wanted was to spin records at a radio station that all my friends listened to. That's all. Community is what I wanted, though I would have issued a quick **"blow me"** if anybody had put it to me using those particular words.

My very first job in radio was an internship at WRKO in Boston, a pretty good rock station. People always ask me, "How do you get started in radio?" I say do what I did: Go to a radio station and say you'll do anything. And then, do anything. For me, doing anything meant working as an intern in the station's news department.

This was 1976, and the first thing I learned was the importance of preparation. Every day my job was to cut up pieces of taped news sound bites and write five different separate news items around each segment.

My internship hours were six to ten at night, but I'd come in every day at two and not leave until eleven so I could learn as much as I could as quickly as possible. Apprenticing myself to everyone at the station, I learned how to massage the news into a radio-ready text from people whose politics were so far to the right of mine that I could barely believe I sat in the same room with them. But I shut my mouth, listened, and learned more about news gathering then you'd figure out after five years at the Columbia School of Journalism.

I didn't really want to be a hard news person, but I knew it was a way to sidestep into sports. My first on-air job at that station was doing the news, but the reason I wanted the gig was that sports came on after news—and I figured I could practice and maybe get on at times with the scores and some analysis.

I did that for a year and a half, learned a few chops, then decided to search for something more permanent. Ultimately, I headed out to Cape Cod, where I spun records for three years at the best radio station I ever worked at. It was station **WLOM,** and I was the overnight disc jockey at a soft rock album station that specialized in playing six or eight cuts off an album.

Phil Redo and Larry King, the station program and music directors, were dubious when I came in for an interview and told them that more than anything I wanted to work the overnight shift. They were suspicious. ***Why would anyone want the lowest paying and lowest prestige gig on the entire radio?***

The main reason I was hungry for that job was that it was a gig on the radio. Now that I'd been out of the business for a few months, I was desperate to get back in. Even though I was making $300 a week back in Boston doing some bullshit non-radio job that I don't even wish to recall, I was willing to work for the $125 a week that WLOM would pay. I just wanted to be part of a station again, and Phil and Larry were impressed with my missionary zeal. I was hired. **HOO-WAH*!***

It was a dream job, and sometimes I'd hang around after my graveyard shift ended in the morning in order to deliver that day's sports highlights. My break came one morning when the guy who usually wrote up the sports copy was late to work because of car trouble. I wrote up the copy myself, and when the sports guy finally came in, I showed him my copy, afraid he might be threatened.

Summer 1979—the WLOM staff. From left to right: Albert, Larry King, me, Phil Redo, Maureen, and Paul.

"You actually wrote this?" he said, stunned at how good my writing was. Yes, I said. I'd always known I could write, but it felt great to actually get encouragement. And from that moment on, Phil Redo kept urging me onward and upward with my sports radio jones.

What made that radio station so remarkable wasn't just the fact that it was the most popular and hip spot on the dial on Cape Cod. Rather, what made the entire experience so memorable to me was that everybody who worked there always got along, supported one another, and were honest-to-God friends.

I became very close to Larry and Phil and a dozen other folks at the station, and these friendships have endured with the decades. All of us have gone on to be very successful in the radio business in one form or another, but we've always managed to stay grounded to one another.

I still remember our news director saying it's not very often that you can work with a group of people you actually like, let alone *love*. But that's how it was: We all loved one another, and have remained close friends ever since.

We made it the most popular station around, but of course it was eventually sold out from under us. So one midnight in 1980, another van pulled up and out piled a new crew of personnel to take our jobs and station. You can scream and shout all you want, but you'd better learn to roll with the punches in this business.

To be honest, I hadn't actually learned at this point the important lesson of the fragility of radio stations and staff. All I knew back then was that my entire stock of friends and I were now standing out in the cold, literally, and I didn't know how to handle the anger or sadness.

My first time getting my station sold out from under me was very hard emotionally, but the hideousness of losing my job and adopted family at the same moment proved very useful to me in the end. The experience, though utterly wrenching, toughened me up for every other time I would be canned by some **faceless asshole** in some faraway corporate headquarters.

Collecting at the unemployment office, Cape Cod, 1980. From left to right: Albert, Paul, me, and Kathleen.

With my Cape Cod radio station and little utopian community dead, I decided to head to New York in search of a station willing to hire a young woman unafraid to tell her bosses to go fuck themselves. I always thought that New York was the pinnacle, that it was the one place where it was always happening in life and in radio, which in my mind were one and the same thing.

I wanted to put the words **"New York"** on my résumé, and I didn't give a good **HOO-WAH!** what kind of station I worked at. It didn't even bother me when I couldn't land a full-time gig anywhere in New York. All I needed for my fiendish plan to work was a few hours on-air a week in the Big Apple so on paper my credentials would sparkle.

What I ended up getting was the weekend overnight shift at WTFM in New York. So every Saturday morning I would take a train from Boston to New York. From there it was right to the radio station, where I'd work overnight as a disc jockey until six in the morning. Then I'd reverse my route back to Boston, already feeling the glow of one bearing a résumé that was beginning to look as if it might be worth reading.

Later, I also got a full-time job at WBOS in Boston. It was another overnight job, and the bosses couldn't understand why I was so enthused to be working vampire hours. Though that shift is traditionally viewed as the lowest prestige gig on-air, I always loved that dark of the morning time the best.

As always, I like to be left alone to do what I need to do, be it in life or on the radio. I loved that on the overnight shift there's nobody there shuffling between offices and telling you to tidy your work area. *I despise office politics and the assholes who play them,* but that's never a problem overnight. It was just me and a microphone, along with the cranks and insomniacs and the lobster shift out there listening to my theater of the mind.

A glutton for punishment, I then took a third part-time job, this one at WEEI. I was producing pieces, and I was told I'd have to join the appropriate union, which was the Writer's Guild.

Even at this early stage of my development I had amazing self-confidence. I remember one day that the regular sports host at WEEI was sick, and I was stuck in the elevator with two of the people running the station as they decided who should take over producing the show.

"Who can do it?" said one, a stone asshole.

"She can do it," said the other news guy, pointing at me.

"What do you mean she can do it?" he said incredulously.

"You can do that show, right?" he said, turning to me.

"Sure," I said, though I had no idea how to do what was needed. But I figured it out fast.

Still, I was so broke that I couldn't even pay the union's enrollment fee. And as luck would have it, my union went on strike six months after I started there. The problem was in Los Angeles, where the Writer's Guild unit had struck CBS, which also owned my station in Boston.

This was fucked. I wasn't even a writer, and didn't even belong to the union, but I was told that I couldn't go to work. So I stayed out for a couple weeks, and after proving my allegiance to the cause, I was asked to a union meeting at some labor organizer's apartment.

I was even given an assignment on the picket line inside Prudential Center, where our radio station was headquartered. The line was set up around the elevator banks where replacement workers would go up and down from our offices and jobs.

It was just a horrible scene. I watched as the replacements came to work and were met by union members screaming **"scab"** and much worse. It was so horrible that I knew right then that I could never cross a picket line. Besides the humiliation of being a scab, there is the overriding fact that I would never want to be used as a pawn by those assholes who own and run radio stations.

Still, as I like to say, BABY NEEDS A NEW PAIR OF SHOES. I took a job as an airborne traffic reporter operating between Boston and Cape Cod. I would spend Friday, Saturday, Sunday, and Monday in an airplane telling the world about that day's beach or commuter traffic. The job didn't pay very much, but it kept my finger in the business while I tried to figure out what to do with my life. It also allowed me to spend the summer hanging on the Cape. **HOO-WAH!**

After the strike was finally settled, however, a new set of problems began. I'd always suffered from asthma, but my attacks were becoming more frequent and violent. I went into the hospital in Boston, where I began sounding amazingly like Dustin Hoffman's portrayal of Ratso Rizzo in *Midnight Cowboy*.

"Get me to Florida!" I'D TELL ANYONE WHO'D LISTEN. **"Forget everything else, just get me to Florida!"**

It was time to get out of Boston for reasons beyond the fact that I was beginning to wheeze like Ratso Rizzo right before he died.

There was no Jon Voight in my life, but I did have a few complicated relationships in Boston. I was going through a lot personally at the time, and taking a powder now seemed like the best form of diplomacy. Packing only my dog and cat, I said out loud, "AND AWAY WE GO"

And we were off to Florida. I figured I'd work there for a year, boost up my résumé even more, then return to Boston for good. Wrong. I never went back.

I'd heard of an opening in Tampa for a show host on an all-talk station, and they hired me. I rented a bungalow built over somebody's garage just footsteps from the beach. It was heavenly, and I supposed I'd never leave. I bought a boat and squeezed juice from oranges growing on trees in my backyard. WISH YOU WERE HERE, **suckers!**

I worked at the same station in Tampa most of the time I lived in Florida. The place had many different station managers and call letters, but always bore an appealing trace of swamp hoodoo and weirdness.

The station was located in a woebegone culvert off of a bog, and one morning after a shift I opened the door of the station to find an actual alligator staring at me. IT WAS ONLY IN LATER YEARS THAT I REALIZED I WAS LOOKING AT THE EXACT IMAGE OF DON FEHR, THE HEAD OF THE BASEBALL PLAYERS' UNION.

When I first got to Tampa, I learned that absolutely nobody listened to my tiny new station. I was on from eight to eleven every night, and I was supposed to be a general talk host. It was amazing how low-down this station was—I would go on for three hours, and I'd be lucky to get two calls all night. I'd pick up a newspaper and start reading out loud whatever was going on around town or the world. If I was lucky enough to get a call, I'd keep the sucker on for ten minutes just to fill up the time.

I didn't want to talk about taxes or bond issues or that standard talk radio shit that just doesn't interest me. Invariably, I would end up talking about sports. As I chattered, I hoped and prayed that someone at home would be so annoyed by what I was saying that they'd call me up on the air.

This kind of low-down laboring is what really paying your dues is all about. Now, **paying dues** is a concept that kids trying to get into the thrill-a-minute world of radio are no longer interested in. They come off their college alternative radio stations having spun only **Mindless Fucks** records in their lives, and now, having graduated, they want their own show. Pay your dues and get in line, junior.

For me, the horrors of having a show where no one called and there was nothing to talk about was the best education I ever got on how to make the radio sing. Today, I have no fears. Because now, as the Fabulous Sports Babe, I come to work knowing that I'll have a billion people calling today and tomorrow and forever.

What is difficult is to sit there in a pissant Tampa studio for three hours with no one calling. That will teach you something about living and dying on the radio, believe me.

It was while I was at that station that I first learned I could do anything and survive on talk radio. On that one fateful night, my producer had arranged for me to do an hour-long in-studio interview with a local artist who painted two-inch miniature portraits of God knows what.

This genius artist comes on the air, and I had to endure him holding up his ridiculous tiny paintings to his microphone while talking about his art. *This was not, needless to say, good radio.* But I kept it up, his talking about his midget paintings on the radio, and finally the hour was over. It was then that I realized that nobody else on the planet could do this—survive an hour with the most boring man in the world talking about the most ridiculous shit in history.

The Babe, THOUGH STILL UNNAMED, **was alive.**

Seven

Radio Daze

Adventures in the
Sexist Pig-Dog Airstream

*I want to bite the hand that feeds me / I want to bite that
hand so badly / I want to make them wish they'd never seen
me.*

—"Radio, Radio" by Elvis Costello

Radio, IN MANY RESPECTS, **is a sleazy little business.**
Actually, make that a sleazy *huge* business. And despite what the
pooh-bahs of the industry say about radio serving the public interest, any idiot who has spent more than fifteen seconds at any station knows there is only one thing that this medium is really
about: **MAKING MONEY.** Lots and lots of dough. That's the
moral to the radio story, kiddies, and if you don't like its smell,
then get out of the fucking kitchen.

Now if this sounds like I'm bitter about the business that has
made me as rich as the sultan of Brunei, then please be most gra-
cious and come over to Mother's dinette and blow me. Because
I'm not bitter, just realistic.

I've been screwed over during my rise to airstream empress
again and again and again. The names and numbers of the assholes
who played **roulette** with my life are embedded in my memory like a wood sliver under skin. But just because I remember
those hosebags doesn't mean I try and settle grudges.

The best way to settle scores with any nemesis, I know, is to
reflect on the fact that I'm the only person on the planet doing
what I do—and they're stuck in their miserable carcasses while I
am being venerated across the world like Evita Perón. DON'T CRY
FOR ME, PENNSYLVANIA, THE STEELERS WILL BE BACK!

Anyway, where was I—oh yes, **Old Testament revenge.** As

they say, *revenge is a dish best served cold.* And if any one of the millions in the radio business who've ever stuck a knife between the Babe's shoulder blades would like to compare paychecks, eat me, I don't have time.

I just refuse to live in the past. I thought of this precept recently while I was browsing through a friend's library. Almost all of her books were about **codependency** or **Twelve Step recovery** or **crystals** or **healing** or *holistic something or other.* Paging through the books, I was struck by how each volume began by dealing with how people who have been traumatized can heal themselves.

These unfortunates, the books detailed, have gone through this and gone through that. They've been abused, beaten, ignored, and neglected. But on the last page of each and every one of these books there is always the message **"So what?"**

What up wit' dat is that it doesn't matter how screwed over you've been through your life until now. You still get up. You still get a job. You still get a haircut. You still get a goddamn life. That's your responsibility as a grown-up, no matter how horrid your life has been so far. CARPE DIEM IS THE KEY; IT MEANS **"seize the day"** IN LATIN, YOU **losers.** More than that, it's the motto Babe lives her life by every second of every day. **HOO-WAH!**

I don't have time for recriminations, because I barely have time to do my laundry. Still, the Babe's enduring success, I've had to learn sometimes about leaving people behind. It's never been something I've been good at, because I've never had an extended family to practice upon.

It's hard realizing that not everyone I knew from the old days is ecstatic about my success and fame. I'm not just talking about people in the radio business, but some old friends whom I thought were outside of the bullshit everyday showbiz melodrama.

I've had people I've known for twenty years say, "Oh, you've changed, you think you're a big deal now." Bullshit. I don't think I'm a big deal, and nothing I've ever done has indicated that my head has swelled any bigger than when I was a hustling twenty-year-old just trying to get anyone to give me a job in front of a microphone.

If my success has made some people I've known from the old days feel uncomfortable, that's too bad. It's not my fault that they're exactly where they were twenty years ago. There's a lot of jealousy inside and outside of this business, and all I have to do to remind myself of my triumph over impossible odds is to repeat this mantra: "No one else is doing this, no one else is doing this."

And yet, because I do a radio show that's heard all over the country, many people still assume that I think I'm some big deal who really believes she's Princess Di. **I'm not now, nor will I ever be, Princess Di.**

To be sure, living with "The Fabulous Sports Babe Show" is fun. But I will never know how big it is or exactly how many stations are buying it. I never ask to know the exact number of the millions of listeners who visit Pizza Hut and I think I'd be frightened if I found out.

I am not the kind of person who will allow herself to know this supposedly essential shit. I don't bother because this type of information won't do me any good except to clog my brain with details that don't matter. What matters is what the Babe says and does, and the issues on which she speaks out. The rest is just fodder for the number crunchers. I can read a room and tell what is needed to satisfy my fans, but once you start pandering to what those bean counters want, you lose your soul as well as your creative spirit.

I will always retain my humility, BECAUSE I AM NOT A **prick.** One of my stock phrases on the show is about how I'm hosting this show because "the other ninety-nine people they called weren't home." On some level I believe that, though I know it's not true. It's just my way of telling my **Babe-enslaved fans** that though I may debase them, I will never change or forget them.

So above all, I gotta be me. Yes, I understand I can't say the phrase **"fucking bastards"** on radio. Still, I do enjoy saying the similar sounding nonsense phrase **"farging bastadges"** over and over on the air. What are they going to do, call the cops?

Babe really came into her own during my time in Tampa. Her attitude, though, wasn't a character, but an extension of me. Needless to say, Babe's persona made some of the suits edgy.

I still remember when I was doing sports reports for a show in Tampa. I'd been at that station for five years when one day we got a new general manager who came right out and told me that he just wasn't comfortable with a woman delivering the sports. He never told me why he felt this way, he just showed me the door and kicked my ass out. The bastard. **And that's how it's done in this fancy-free radio business, Bubbas.**

During difficult times like that, I always tried to remember how I ever got into this deranged business in the first place. It no longer mattered, of course: Radio was all I knew, and as always, *baby needs shoes.* Still, in the dark moments of my career, I liked to remember the vision.

You see, you bastards, the idea of radio as my way of life first came to me in my early twenties. I had a true and profound VISION of the world to be. Strangely, it was a dream that I didn't understand until five years later.

My **vision** came to me while I was staying upstairs at my Aunt Ruth's place on Cape Cod during the summer of 1974. Aunt Ruth has always been more of a mother to me than anybody else, and I don't think it's a coincidence that heavy truths struck me as I slept in the apartment above her house. It had already been an interesting summer, as I'd completely altered my brain chemistry by ingesting massive amounts of LSD and smoking unbelievable quantities of pot. In truly every sense of the word, I grew up that summer.

Then one night I had a bizarre dream in which I saw a dozen black knoblike things laid out on a strange table before me. I woke up in a sweat, not knowing what this was all about. It completely unsettled me, and the Babe is not easily rattled.

Cut to 1979, five years after I had my dream and three years since I'd gone into radio. I'm working at this great station on Cape Cod, and one day I'm standing at the studio console with my hands on the board. I turned on the microphone to begin my show, and then it hit me.

I looked down. AND THEN I WAS STRUCK DUMB WITH THE REALIZATION THAT THE CONSOLE WITH THE BLACK KNOBS THAT I'D DREAMED ABOUT LONG BEFORE WAS RIGHT HERE, IN FRONT OF ME, FOR REAL. It was crystal clear that this was my exact dream, that I had experienced déjà vu all over again, as Yogi Berra had it. **Thank you Buddha,** *I said, for granting me this time-delayed vision.*

"RADIO, BABE, RADIO," the Lord spake through this vision. I listened to that profound message and never looked back. It was inside that itty-bitty Cape Cod station that I at last realized how much I loved being stuck in that little room that is a radio studio. Inside that tiny room I was finally able to create an entire world for myself.

Every day I remake that world, and those red lights flashing on the telephone bank are the heartbeats of my soul. Inside that universe I can let in as many people as I want—or I can hang up on the bastards. THE POINT IS IT'S MY WORLD, BABY, **cuz it's my fucking show.**

A lot of people in radio or television are in the business primarily for ego gratification. All they really want is for strangers to come up to them in the grocery and say, **"Hey, Mr. Star, I saw you on the tube last night"** or **"Hey, sweetheart, I heard you on the radio this morning."**

I, naturally, am not like the others. I do this job as the Fabulous Sports Babe for me, not so people I don't know will fawn over me in shopping centers. The Babe in her own mind exists only to be in that little radio studio. While it is nice when citizens come up to me and say, "Are you the Babe?" adulation isn't nutritious enough to live on. You need soul.

Sports Radio
950 KJR
We've locked in "The Babe" weekdays 1 to 5 pm.

When people do approach me out in the world I feel extremely shy, believe it or not **you cynical bastards.** But it's the truth—I live for that space inside the airwaves, not the ego rubs. I passionately believe in what I do inside radio's theater of the mind. And because of that, this show is more than just a way for me to make enormous amounts of money while at the same time visiting revenge upon those who have messed with me on my way up. (Though that shit doesn't hurt, let me tell you.)

No, the Babe is art. Both in herself and her show. THIS ISN'T ZSA ZSA TALKING, **it's the Babe. HOO-WAH***!*

The major reason I left Tampa for Seattle was artistic considerations. Rick Scott, the program director for a group of stations up there, began calling me late at night in Florida to ask me to just come visit Seattle. He worked me over for a couple of months, but I just kept putting him off with "What are you, an idiot? Why would I leave Tampa? **Wait a minute, Rick,** YOU'RE GOING TO HAVE TO TALK LOUDER **because I've got Bain de Soleil** IN MY EAR!"

THE FABULOUS SPORTS BABE

Finally, Rick bullshitted me into taking a trip up to Washington. It was the Fourth of July, and all these Seattle radio geeks were sitting out on Lake Union and schmoozing me. It was so beautiful there that day— there were sea planes coming out of an ocean-blue sky and big salmon broiling on the barbie.

Rick Scott, of course, was also there. For the rest of the afternoon the two of us talked about different philosophies of radio. We both talked of the public service aspect—something, as I've mentioned before, you'll never hear discussed by almost anybody in radio at any time. And then I explained to Rick how I approached my own program as a rock and roll show, not just as another jerk-off chatfest.

That said, I then told Rick it was time for me to get the hell out of Seattle and back home to Tampa, where the good life lives. Which is exactly what I did. When I got home and turned on my answering machine, I heard the voice of Rick Scott telling me *"if you don't come to Seattle, you'll never know how good you can be."*

Hmmmmmmm. I thought about that message, and played it again. Without that message I would never have left and taken that job in Seattle. Rick Scott is still a very important person in my life, and I would like to thank him for that, ya bastard!

But that bastard saw something in me that he recognized could be historic. He was also quite open about the realities that would be waiting for me in Seattle. He told how the entire town was composed of tree-hugging granola heads whose favorite sentence was **"Let's sit down and have a latte."**

Rick Scott also told me that his sad-sack town had never before had an aggressive, confrontational talk radio show host like me. A large percentage of the populace, he promised, was going to absolutely hate me from the first second they heard the dulcet tones of *moi*. I had to be ready.

Yes, he told me, the station would take some heat for my early performances. But I was the one, he said, who was going to take the brunt of the bullshit that rained down upon Seattle when I first began my Babe reeducation seminars on the public. While the rest of the radio stations in town were doing *nice-guy radio,* I prepared myself to become the first, best, and only in-your-face radio personality Seattle had ever seen.

"This is a task very few people would want to take on in Seattle," Rick Scott told me. "Because when you do take on this role, everybody is going to hate you in this town."

And they did. **Half the people in Seattle still hate my ass.** But Rick Scott understood the vision of my show, and fought all the good fights on my behalf. For the first six months I was in town the station salespeople were having fits with him because of the way I was behaving on the air. The station's general manager was beside himself with what had blown in from Florida with just the wrong amount, he felt, of **sarcasm and badass-edness.** Rick, at times, would block the studio door

It only looks like I'm miserable in tree-hugging granola land—actually, this is Portage Bay Glacier in Alaska, not Hooterville.

from that cretin who was trying to tone me down. But the cretin saw the light and now runs a radio group, and my show is on a bunch of his stations.

"You can't go in there!" he'd say, literally putting his 6'6" frame in the doorway to keep the suit out. Others came to bitch, and Rick blocked them out, too—the out-of-their-minds idiots who thought the world would explode because I'd said this or that.

Rick was the only one telling me to keep pushing the envelope, to break Babe past anything I'd ever dreamed for her. He spun the cocoon that brought the Fabulous Sports Babe to the next level.

It helped, of course, that Rick Scott was correct in believing in my talent. Within weeks of arriving in Seattle, all the newspapers and television stations were doing stories on me, and the city seemed ready to explode with **Babe-mania.** In what seemed moments, I had turned that town on its ear.

Now, with all that dreamy reach-for-the-stars-girl stuff behind us, I must also point out that THE RADIO BUSINESS IS AS **tough** AND **cold-blooded** AS THE SPORTS BUSINESS. I always thought that when I got out of local radio I'd be through dealing with all the small-minded idiots who ran whatever station I was working for. What I've found, however, is that idiots exist on all levels—as do geniuses.

If you want a good insight into show business—a category in which I include radio—you might want to read *The Late Shift* by Bill Carter. It's about the battle between David Letterman and Jay Leno for Johnny Carson's vacant couch. The battle at the top of this showbiz mountain, the world soon learned, was as ridiculous as anything going on at a forty-watt radio station in **Dipstick, Idaho.**

In one scene, Jay Leno is hiding in a closet in order to eavesdrop on negotiations. It worked—Leno got the information that he needed and was offered the job.

The way the book resonated most with me was in its description of how the bosses of showbiz never tell the talent anything. The moguls of this business always tell the talent whatever the talent wants to hear. They do this because they believe us to be spoiled children. They tell you they're your friend, and the next thing you know you're sending your tape and résumé off to a Ham radio outfit in Anchorage, Alaska.

That's show—and radio—business. If you don't like it, or can't take it, do something else. There's an element of sleaze in every business, and radio is no different. ***You just have to accept that this is the way it is . . . like boxing.***

The odd thing is that no matter how big you get in this business, everyone acts like they're doing you a big favor just to let you on the air. The bosses think they're giving you an opportunity, but in truth, no one has given the Babe an opportunity in years. I did it myself, my own way.

Today I also endure the added pressure of knowing that my national show generates several zillions of dollars' worth of revenue every year. There's a lot of dough riding on the Fabulous Sports Babe, and that's all the radio business is really about: money.

I don't just mean I've got advertisers like **Joe's Jockstraps** counting on me. I'm also fully aware that a lot of individuals are relying on me. These are people who work on or for "The Fabulous Sports Babe Show," and whose careers are on the line with the life or death of my program.

I also feel I'm working on behalf of the many women in other businesses who've gone out of their way to contact and encourage me. I've heard from, among others, a woman running a record company, another working at CBS Sports, and a third operating her own computer software business. All got in touch with me just to say that they were with me in my quest and that they wanted me to succeed. **HOO-WAH!**

That is just great, but I realize that with this comes all the attendant and inevitable bullshit. I also know that I simply can't allow myself to fail at this. I just can't. There are too many people riding on the Babe spaceship, and I don't just mean folks who I write checks to. No, I also know I have a responsibility to people from afar who are rooting for me to succeed in a place where women never have before.

IN RADIO, YOU'RE JUST BOUND TO GET FIRED **no matter how good you are.** It's the nature of the business—and 99 percent of the time that you're canned it has nothing to do with you.

When you get screwed in this business, just consider it another graduation.

Eight
Radio Daze II

I Become the Babe-raham Lincoln of Sports Talk

And the radio/is in the hands/of such a lot of fools . . .
—**"Radio, Radio" by Elvis Costello**

My favorite on-air stunt I ever pulled occurred in Tampa with the unveiling of the infamous **BARTMOBILE.** The point of the Bartmobile was to grab baseball commissioner Bartlett Giamatti's learned attention in a manner both ridiculous and sublime. What we wanted to do was send a lowbrow message to the highbrow former president of Yale that Tampa both deserved and was in dire need of a Major League Baseball team.

A club of our own had been Tampa's holy grail since  was still pitching, and I decided to help out in ways beyond pissing and moaning on the radio. So under my direction, my station bought this 1984 crusty and crazy shit Oldsmobile with a diesel engine and the battered look of a scuttled battleship.

We called the monstrosity the Bartmobile, and the car began making public appearances at Tampa shopping malls and grocery stores. There, local citizens were invited to sign the car in indelible ink. The Bartmobile would be a rolling petition pleading for a big league team for Tampa.

The car would then be delivered by me to the baseball commissioner himself. In a lavish presentation ceremony, we planned for Giamatti to be given the petitions—as well as the keys and registration of the Bartmobile.

People went absolutely nuts over the Bartmobile in Tampa,

and we got 42,000 people to sign the plea—one signature for every seat in the city's Thunderdome stadium.

And then, out of the blue, Bart Giamatti died. I was stunned. I remember cursing the Lord with "this guy has got to die on me right in the middle of my biggest promotion ever? He has to *die*? Can anything else go wrong in my life?" OK, so I'm not exactly suffering the slings and arrows that Job endured, but did the key guy in my best ever promotion have to croak?

Well, of course, we had to rename the Bartmobile the **"Baysball Machine,"** and our campaign continued. It was an important mission to me.

Finally, it was time to drive the goddamn thing to the 1989 World Series in San Francisco. Faye Vincent, Giamatti's successor as commissioner, would be holding court there, and it was time, I decided, to drop off the goods.

So two guys—the original **Heckyl** and **Jeckyl** from my show—drove the barge out west, where I met up with them and prepared for our moment of glory. Sadly, Faye had been tipped off to our scheme. **The bastard!**

Vincent spent the whole series dodging me, fully aware that I planned to drop the Baysball Machine's keys in his hand. Knowing he was being stalked for a photo op, Faye just didn't want to see me at all. If ever I caught a glimpse of him during the World Series, Faye would immediately run and hide. He wasn't keen on my grandiose bullshit on behalf of Tampa baseball, but we planned to continue to torment the commissioner with the Baysball Machine until he gave in and gave Tampa a team.

My mission for Tampa continued even when I left town for Seattle. The Seattle Mariners were teetering, and I promised my friends in Florida that I would work the **Babe magic** and bring that woebegone Washington State team to Tampa. True, I would now be in the far more dangerous role as a ***deep undercover double secret agent*** while I was in Seattle. But I had my vow to my Tampa hordes, and I meant to keep it.

(FYI, and up yours baseball, I would have never believed that it would take until 1998 before a Major League Tampa franchise would play an inning. But I've already purchased four season tickets to the Tampa Bay Devil Rays right behind the dugout. As soon as I retire, which may not be that far away, I will simply put my feet atop that dugout and watch the rest of my life float by.)

When I got to Seattle I quickly discovered that I was working with the laziest people I'd ever met. Most of the on-air personalities in town would sit at home all day smoking pot and listening to my show. Then they'd come in that afternoon or night to work their shifts, and all they'd do was regurgitate what I'd just said earlier that day. **Bastards!**

Seattle was a **fucked-up backwater town** when I first got there, and I like to think I was responsible for dragging that poor city into the future. What about **Kurt Cobain** or **Bill Gates,** you may ask? I WAS **bigger**. I had more fun in Seattle than either of those squares. I never had to wear a tie to work, and I didn't have to hang with **Courtney Love.**

But man, if you could have seen what was up when I arrived from Tampa. I remember I'd just gotten to town when I turned on the big local Seattle news and talk radio station in the middle of the day. What I heard was a host discussing chrysanthemums. He was giving a seminar on *flower arrangement!* Unbelievable!

I couldn't believe it. Was I in the country's 12th largest market or its 212th? IT'S ELEVEN A.M., **and this guy is discussing GARDENING!** The talk show host was on a monster radio station, we were in the middle of an election year, and he couldn't think of anything heavier to discuss than soil science? *What God-forsaken place have I moved to?* I wondered as I unpacked my bags with a heavy heart and daydreamed of Tampa.

But I showed up for work, and immediately saw what I had to do. I've been the lead dog at every station I've ever worked for, and when they gave me the keys to that place I determined that it was time to **ROCK AND ROLL.** The ratings for my time period went up tenfold within moments of my arrival, and I can assure you it wasn't because we were discussing origami on the air.

The town ate it up, even the sizable contingent of listeners who loathed me. I would even make fun of the station sometimes. Callers would ask why my time slot wasn't expanded, but Christ, who can do more than four hours a day? Everyone wants to rip their boss, but only the Babe can do it. My persona is big enough to get away with it. *HOO-WAH!*

Me enjoying the only sunny day in Hooterville.

I made a career while I was in Seattle hating the town on the air. I'd get on and just talk about how in the world did I ever get stuck living here in **Hooterville,** a town filled with the dumbest people in the world? To be honest, I believed it. **Except for Seattle's coffee, which is truly great, and its place as the historic birthplace of JIMI HENDRIX, that town is a hopeless zero.**

That said, I still bear my bent form of loyalty to that goofy town. There were many things I had to educate Seattle about, and as all good teachers know, you can't help but care the deepest for your most idiotic students.

My first reclamation project in Seattle concerned the town's building up a proper hatred for nearby **Portland.** Now, when I grew up as a Boston fan, we all believed in the sanctity of great hates and grudges with other cities and their evil teams. The closest team geographically to the Boston Red Sox were the New York Yankees, and unless you were a total pinhead you knew that if you were a Bosox fan you simply loathed and despised and spit at the mere mention of New York or the Yankees. We knew Yankee fans hated us just as much, which was the way it was supposed to be. **HATING YOUR NEIGHBORS** IS AS AMERICAN AS **cherry pie,** to quote my old canasta partner and pal H. Rap Brown.

Anyway, I come to Seattle and discover that despite the fact that Portland was our closest major city, only three hours from my ass, they were not hated in my newly adopted hometown. No, hating is not thought proper in Seattle, **tabernacle** OF THE **politically correct.** And so, even though we were living in a big metropolitan center, everybody in town had that New Age attitude of love thy neighbor that comes with being a granola-loving tree-hugging asshole.

It was very annoying to go to basketball games when the **Portland Trailblazers** would come play the **Supersonics** in Seattle. At every game I noticed that the Sonics fans just sat on their hands. Portland would come in, slap around the hometown team, and then leave. Time and again, and one more time for good measure, they'd kick our asses.

This was still a satisfactory situation for most people in Seattle. Everyone I talked to in town would say, "Yes, the Trailblazers come in and kick our asses in our own arena every game, but that is OK. The Trailblazers are from the Great Northwest, just like us, and we should be nice to them."

My attitude was: No, we shouldn't be nice to them. **They're the goddamn enemy.** Portland shouldn't come into our house and make fools of us and not pay the karmic debt, I told my astonished audience of listeners who weren't used to such tough talk from a voice on the air.

Babe's Best Bets

The Babe is predicting that those great minds in Portland, where the Rose Garden Arena was christened without all the seats having been installed, will decide to remove *every* seat so that for each game they can claim standing room only.

Give us the chrysanthemum man, some listeners cried. But I wouldn't. I was the Fabulous Sports Babe, and they needed to learn. On the air, I couldn't stop pointing out and embarrassing my own town with evidence of how lame they were as fans. Every time Portland came to Seattle for a basketball game, their loyalists probably outnumbered Sonics rooters by nine thousand to six thousand. Coming to Seattle was like a home game for the Blazers.

Well, I wasn't going to allow this bullshit to go on. *So I encouraged fans* TO THROW BEER ON THE **Blazers.** If they were going to kick our asses, at least we should make them feel like they didn't enjoy coming here. *HOO-WAH!*

This actually became a cause that an entirely new community embraced. This is what people in the media need to do—help disconnected people see and feel the community breathing around them. We teach the people, and they will follow.

So we began our program, simple in its original execution, like the **PEACE CORPS.** First, we taught people that if they were driving to a Sonics game and saw anybody with an Oregon license plate, they should give the trespassers the finger. To further incite them, I began calling Portland **"Pixley,"** the backwater village next to **"Hooterville."** I built up a proper feeling of loyalty in a town that had never really rooted in their heart for any team, any time. In a lot of ways, I feel that my greatest legacy from my stint in Seattle was that there is now a rivalry with Portland that wasn't there before. I am very proud of that.

Oh, let me not forget another lasting legacy of my time in Seattle. During my assault on the Trailblazers, I began referring to Portland as the **"PLUMBER'S BUTT of America,"** and it stuck. It is a phrase I continue to use with mirth and truth on my national show. If anyone in Portland feels disputatious about this designation, please join me in inviting your bad selves to step behind the curtain and blow me.

Again, my on-air persona is not just showtime bluster that I put on and take off. My station manager in Seattle came up to me once and said that who I am in real life is just a slicker version of the Babe I am on the radio. Get outta town, I told him, who I am is no more slick than anything I've ever laid on the radio audience.

In real life, I do go around saying, **"Blow me, YOU FUCK."** And that's the way I am on the radio—you just don't hear what I say while I'm pushing the edit button. If some asshole on the phone swears at me, I'll say "fuck you" right back. Sometimes these idiots will call and complain to ESPN, but nobody heard it on the air, so I'm safe. Or say somebody makes a generic idiotic comment. I'll close him out, then push the edit button. "Hey Jerry," I'll tell the caller, "do me a favor."

Triumphant tour of the "Plumber's Butt of America," Portland, Oregon, at the Nike headquarters.

Nike remote in Portland, 1995—me and ex-Laker
Michael Thompson.

"What?" Jerry will say, still thinking the whole world is listening.

"Blow me!" And then I click off. I'm very good at this. **Don't FUCK *with the Babe.***

My act that really wasn't an act bowled the town over. My station in Seattle had been riding on very hard times for a very long time, and they needed something that had never been heard in those parts, or any parts. And as I said, the rest of the people at that station didn't do anything. I single-handedly put that station on my back and carried them up to the mountaintop. I was the only talent at that place who put myself out and dared to offend and be controversial. Meanwhile, as I'm making this station rich, I was put through hell for my first six months because idiot tree-huggers were complaining to station management that I was saying "HELL" and "damn" on their precious airwaves.

Everybody else at that station—and at most radio sports talk shows—just want to sit in their little chairs and pretend they're the guy sitting next to you on the barstool watching a game. Well screw all of you, that's not who the Fabulous Sports Babe is.

Here's the "Sonic Cynic," the bane of Hooterville and my favorite caller because he pissed everyone off. He lost a bet and we got to shave his head.

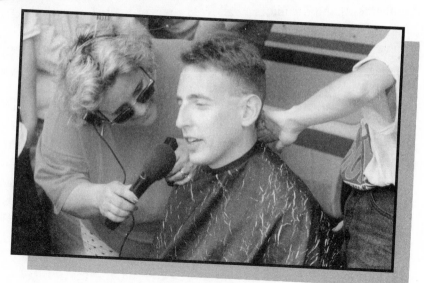

Then, after I remade their station and became famous in one more town, those idiots in Seattle wouldn't let me go on to be a national superstar. I still remember when the offer came in to me to do a big-time radio show on ESPN and the general manager of my station decided to be a hard-on about setting me free. A normal guy would have been proud to have launched one of his own employees to a national show, but this putz said to me, "I own you. I'll decide where you go."

Well bite me. I can't tell you what A MAJOR **pain-in-the-ass**

HASSLE evolved when I announced my intention to leave Seattle for ESPN. The people who ran that local station were small-time nobodies who thought that because they lived in Seattle they were some big deal and that the rest of the world should come kiss their asses. For four months ESPN had negotiated in good faith with KJR on a buyout of my contract. After agreeing to release me to ESPN the Seattle station decided to be pricks about my leaving, at which point I contacted Jeff Smulyan, owner of the Seattle Mariners and owner of Emmis Broadcasting. Jeff informed me that the first thing I needed to do was get agent Lisa Miller and second was that he'd get me the right attorney. Within forty-eight hours Lisa was on board and Jeff had directed me to Bill Cronin, the finest lawyer in the land. Bill laid a trap on KJR station management, and the idiots swallowed the bait hook, line, and sinker.

The management made the mistake of taking me off the air, eventually rendering my contract null and void. **Bad Move, guys, you should have read the contract.** In the interim, I spent the next three months in Hawaii on their dime, sending frequent postcards back to my bosses in Seattle telling them how I wished they were with me. **HOO-WAH!**

The Seattle station kept saying that they had made me famous, which was bullshit. Seattle didn't make me. If anything, I put Seattle on the map. **I was the queen, the EMPRESS, the all-powerful Babe.** When Dan Rather's CBS News program came to town to do a story on how the Mariners had just been bought by Japanese interests, they naturally approached me for quotes. When the story ran on the nightly news, it was the Fabulous Sports Babe telling the world what time it was in Seattle.

However, the real moment I knew I'd arrived as a major force in the airstream was the day I learned I'd been sued for $50,000 by a seventy-year-old man who claimed I had beaten him up at the Seattle Kingdome. Alas, another goober for Bill Cronin to knock off. The claim was utter bullshit. Since the case was ridiculous and frivolous, after filing the claim the lawsuit was dropped. Apparently, the little old man realized that the notion that I had "beat him up" was going to be impossible to prove, particularly since I was nowhere near the incident.

Of course, the more successful I became the more people wanted to take the credit for my success. Those who were assholes along the way, the ones who stood out for being unhelpful at every turn, were, of course, the first to take bows. You know the kind—middle-management types who spent their entire time with an organization hassling you. Now that you're in the big time, they are the same assholes who want all the credit and honor for having sprung you to the show.

I always remember. It was funny when we went back to Seattle to broadcast from the Final Four tournament a couple years after my tussle to get out of Seattle and go national. The shows were great—on the show we billed our journey to Seattle as Babe's triumphant return to the dumb-ass town she put on the map. We just totally ragged the city, which was a lot of fun. It was a joke, but half the city seemed to think that we were seriously dumping on them. **DUPES! Dopes!**

The beauty part came after one of our Seattle broadcasts, when the asshole who made my life such hell when I wanted to go to ESPN and leave his operation came up to me with a big cheery greeting and a boot-licking grin. This guy who'd previously told me he owned me now came up and said, "I miss you."

I looked at him, this pale excuse for a man, and sneered. He'd failed his lesson in Babe-ocracy. **"You *should* miss me,"** I **said.** *"I was the best thing that ever happened to you."*

"Babe, I miss you," he said again, pleading, as I placed him in my mind at the front of the line for the karmic guillotine.

My main commandment is just as much in effect with radio station general managers as with idiot phone callers: **THE BABE IS ALWAYS RIGHT,** *and* **don't fuck with the Babe.** I don't know if the people at ESPN knew this when they hired me: You can't hire the Fabulous Sports Babe and then expect her to change. I can't do it. Like Popeye, **I yam what I yam.**

Even when some of the people at the network started to knock what I was doing on my show at the beginning, I was quite firm. I told them that I had gotten here because of what I do, and that if certain entities here didn't like what I did, too bad. They should have never hired me.

That said, there have been several distinctive people who have stood up for me at ESPN since virtually the very first day. Prime among them have been Chris Berman, known around here as Boomer, though I liken him to ELVIS. Chris is the rock star of his generation, and as the most known and loved face on ESPN, I imagine his kisser will one day be deservedly plastered as an add-on to Mount Rushmore.

Chris truly *is* ELVIS. I've seen him in airports when fans mob him, want him, can't get enough of his brilliance. He could be making millions a year on some network full-time, but he's chosen to spend his entire career at ESPN. He is a fabulous guest, and when he comes on the show every Friday during the football season, I don't even bother taking calls: Boomer is entertainment enough for all.

I've known Chris since 1985, when the Super Bowl was in Tampa and I was a radio rat scrambling for some usable tape. I'm not stupid—I'd made up my mind a long time before that I would get to know and interact on a first-name basis with all these big

Me and Elvis (actually Chris Berman). They broke the mold when they made this guy.

national wheels in the business. And you know, when the big job at ESPN came through, guess who was there for me? Chris Berman. He is one of the most supportive people I know, and I know he's been the same for other ESPN women like Robin Roberts and Linda Cohn.

I still remember something Chris said my second day on the job. He was walking out the door after coming in to say hello, and then stopped, turned around, and looked me straight in the eye. God, it gave me a chill to see Elvis himself staring me down. **"We're counting on you,"** Boomer said, very soberly.

"Don't worry," I told him, and that's exactly how I feel.

I also absolutely adore ESPN's Sportscenter anchor and boxing expert **Charlie Steiner.** Charlie, of course, is a completely different animal than Chris Berman. On the surface, Charlie seems like a staid, highly educated sports historian and philosopher. But he also has a wonderful sense of humor. Most important, Charlie is almost always available to be a guest on my radio or television programs.

While these guys are doing me a favor by coming on my program, I also think my show serves to humanize fellows like Chris and Charlie, whose images are sometimes frozen in their jobs. By coming on my show and putting up with my bullshit, these guys make it possible for us to make them more approachable than they might seem behind their anchor desks at ESPN.

Recently, Charlie verified the good our show has done for him. He told me that even though he's essentially anchored the 6:30 Sportscenter for ten years, he's had more people come up to him in airports and say, "I saw you on the Babe show!" in the last year than he's had approach him in the all the years before. You're a king, Charlie.

Charlie, of course, was a king long before I ever got here. But what I've found especially rewarding is to be able to turn frequent and previously uncelebrated guests on "The Fabulous Sports Babe Show" into honest-to-God famous people. Perhaps the best example is Jim O'Connell, the college basketball writer for the Associated Press. No one travels more miles or knows more about intercollegiate hoops than Jim. But not until he metamorphosed into **JIM RAT** of "The Fabulous Sports Babe Show" did he find his true celebrity. O'Connell was born again as Jim Rat, a fact we never let him forget.

Others we've brought into the limelight haven't been so good at remembering. Prime among them is Kristin-Jeannette Meyers, the Court TV reporter who came on our show every morning to discuss the O. J. Simpson case. She quickly became the **Law Babe** of the show, and in moments ABC was crawling all over her. So there she went, suddenly too big for "The Fabulous Sports Babe Show," eventually heading to CBS where she replaced Paula Zahn on the morning news show. Fine, Kristin.

I put some of our annoying experts on the air regularly simply because I find them annoying. Number one on that list is **Skip Bayless** of ESPN. People hate him all across the country because he is the biggest booster of Dallas in the galaxy. I like to have Bayless on when I simply want to push my listeners over the edge.

Just as irritating to some is ESPN college football commentator BEANO COOK. "Just what are this guy's credentials?" hundreds of Beano-hating callers have asked over the years. I think Beano bugs people because he calls games straight. That and the fact that he is the greatest Notre Dame ass-kisser in the long and proud tradition of South Bend brownnosers.

But let us not forget **ESPN's Big Daddy** BRENT MUSBURGER. I kid you not, Musburger likes to be called **BIG DADDY.** That or **Big Dog.** There's something very amazing about how Brent transforms himself before he goes on the air. You can talk to him off-camera and he's a completely quiet man shrunk into himself. But when the light goes on, he turns into someone completely different—a beaming post of self-confidence and helpful information.

But, as I said, Chris Berman is really one of my very favorite guests. I am very lucky to get him those Fridays that I do, right after he's finished spending four hours writing his swami predictions and football analyses for television.

His technique is set in stone. On the drive into work that Friday, Chris mulls over what he's written that morning. He gets out of his car, then walks right into the Babe's studio to give his first, best, and just assembled thoughts on that weekend's football games.

Still, some of my favorite moments with Chris on the air have nothing to do with football games that would be happening two days hence. Rather, there's no topic he'd rather talk about than seventies football. Once, Chris and I compared great football teams of the mid-nineties to those of twenty years before. We ended up having a thirty-minute conversation on my show about those great Steelers and Cowboy teams back when. Though I frequently drop the bomb on callers who sit and revel in the past, that day was memorable.

BACKBACKBACKBACKBACKBACK **Chris Berman, back into the future for you.**

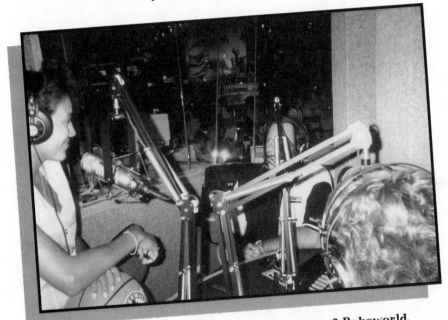

Robin Roberts and Chris Berman at the opening of Babeworld. ESPN calls it ESPN club at Walt Disney World, but Babeaholics everywhere know it's really Babeworld.

Nine

The Babe in Boyland

Sisters are doing it for themselves, you idiot.
—Ancient Chinese hymnal

I always enjoyed playing sports as a kid. I liked being athletic, and carried an appreciation for the bodies, the strength, and the power of sport. I also enjoyed the fact that in athletics, winners and losers were clearly sorted out every day.

So I always paid attention to the peculiar world of competitive games. I learned how to **read the room** of each sport, and came to understand how to tell who was a champion and who was a chump. Naturally, I had a great baseball card collection growing up. But, of course, they were thrown out the first second I was gone.

I played a lot of ball back when I was ten and eleven. I was a pretty good athlete, and I know I could have been a whole lot better. But as a girl, naturally, I wasn't given a lot of encouragement. There wasn't one person in my life saying, **"Do more."** No one cared if I could jump any higher. I'm not making myself out to be a martyr here, just pointing out what it was like to be growing up female in the late sixties and early seventies.

We girls were brought up to observe, not participate. Maybe that's why I'm so good as an adult at describing, commenting on, or talking about sports. Growing up, this was as close to the action as girls were supposed to get. Our place was on the sidelines, cheering or weeping.

Despite the barriers, I kept playing sports as long as I could. **HOW, MY PARENTS WONDERED,** had they ever **spawned THIS FABULOUS SPORTS BABE? HOO-WAH!**

My family just never learned to READ THE **fucking** ROOM and understand that sports was what I truly wanted to do. I wasn't rebelling, I just always wanted to run, jump, and compete.

Compete? That's not what girls are supposed to do, my family thought. I might as well have told them that I'd decided to join a cult of Satan worshipers as announce my intention to go for a college basketball scholarship. Still, in fairness to the people who made me, they weren't alone in their attitude. In their generation, it just wasn't proper to be a woman athlete.

Things have gotten much better, but I think we all might remember that it wasn't until the mid-eighties that it was OK for women to really pursue their sports professionally. By "professionally" I don't just mean that they were now able to make actual sackfuls of cash. I mean it wasn't until a decade ago that a woman could unapologetically train as seriously as a man in a quest to be a world-class athlete.

Martina Navratilova was the pioneer who taught us all that women athletes were willing to seriously train as never before. Martina was the key person to send the message to women: It was finally OK to run, lift weights, and pump the Nautilus equipment.

Chris Evert learned that lesson after her first retirement, and when she came back she'd learned to train. Can you imagine if some woman athlete in the seventies had lifted weights or trained to be a hardbody? They would have burned her as a witch, **Bubba.**

Women sports reporters, meantime, have always been treated as dog shit by the completely **testosterone-charged** sports world. Even now I get looks from people at stadiums who don't think I should be covering sports simply because I'm a woman. I can still remember when I was living in Tampa, covering the worst professional football team in the league. I did this for eight years, and I can't tell you how many times I was hassled and then pulled out of the press line for a gratuitous credentials check. Meantime, standing with me in line would be twenty male reporters who were never, ever accosted.

All I ever wanted was to get in, do my job, and get out. I'd be wearing the same credentials as everyone out there, but week in and week out the rent-a-cops would pull me out of line, check my pass, and tell me that I had the wrong credentials. In their small minds—and remember this is only 1983—they thought the only reason a woman would want to go into the locker room was to ogle naked guys.

SURELY, THESE **lobotomy** OUTPATIENTS WITH BADGES THOUGHT, YOU COULDN'T ACTUALLY BE ACCREDITED *if you're a woman.* Fuck you, I said. Countless times I ended up banging and kicking on the door of a locked locker room after a game. I wanted in, needed in, because this is what I did for a living, and I wasn't going to let some demented macho men stop me from paying my rent.

But stop me they would. If I wanted to interview a player for a radio sound bite, I had to wait outside that damn door. I still remember watching those ignorant redneck sportswriters on those little papers from assorted Hootervilles walking in like kings, the bastards. Those **pencil-pushers** never stuck up for my right to be in that locker room, because most of them also thought that if you were a woman you shouldn't be there in the first place. They had no compunctions about keeping me from doing my job.

I had to put up with that bullshit for years and years. Why? 'Cause a girl's gotta eat. To hell with these idiots, I said, I've still gotta pay the bills. I never thought about not doing this, because radio was the only thing that was paying the landlord.

Oddly, some of the stupidest people hurting the cause were female. I still remember this woman in Tampa who did the sports on TV. She refused to ever go into the locker room because, as she once told me, **"that's not a woman's place."**

Of course, she had three television producers to do all her work, whereas I was alone with a microphone and a prayer, and I had to get that goddamn sound. I didn't really want to be in a locker room. Who wants to be in a dank room with thyroid cases who patronize you as they slip out of their sweaty jockstraps?

But the locker room is where the story is, and if I didn't get in there and get my sound, I'd be eating Kraft macaroni and cheese for the rest of my life. "You don't get it," I told the Tampa television twinkie who continued to insist that it wasn't my "place" to be near these athletes.

Lisa Olsen, of course, is the name that springs to mind when thinking of women sports reporters being treated like trash in the locker room. Olsen was the reporter for the *Boston Herald* who was harassed and humiliated by naked members of the New England Patriots after a game. Her life was destroyed and she had to flee Boston, while the goddamn Patriots never even bothered to pay the fine the league levied against them, the bastards.

The Lisa Olsen case is the most grievous, graphic, and well-publicized incident of sexual harassment in the locker room. The sick part is that this kind of bullshit happened before, will happen again, and is probably happening right now. As long as there are women reporters in locker rooms there will be unprofessional athletes.

The worst incident of harassment I was involved in occurred at the 1985 United States Football League championship held in Tampa. George Allen's Arizona team was playing Philadelphia, and dozens of reporters had gathered in the locker room for a postgame interview with Greg Landry, Arizona's quarterback.

I was walking toward the pack when I was accosted by some 6'6" monster who started forcefully pushing me back. **"You're all a bunch of whores!" he started yelling. "You bitches! You only want one thing, and we got it!"**

I remember thinking that if there was ever a time when I should keep my mouth shut, this was it. So this jerk kept pushing and screaming, and within seconds we had a genuine scene on our hands. None of the all-male reporters came to my rescue, though several did come and surround me and the caveman and begin taking notes. Thanks, guys!

The kicker to this whole incident IS THE IDENTITY OF THE GUY GIVING ME SUCH A HARD TIME. **He was George Allen's chauffeur. His GODDAMN driver!**

It was so humiliating and so enlightening at the same time. It also reinforced my unheard-of notion of becoming a **Jackie Robinson of radio.** My quest to become the world's first woman to do a national sports talk radio show was not based on vanity. Yes, I am aware of my utter fabulousness, which is apparent to anyone with one eye and half a brain. But sheer ego isn't enough to withstand the slings and arrows of the assholes who run the sportsocracy.

Me in the Airstream. I've conquered the world.

These bastards are almost all middle-aged white men who already own all the money in the world. I DIDN'T NEED TO PUT UP WITH THEIR BULLSHIT **IN ORDER TO BE HAPPY;** I'd never been happier than when I was living on the beach in Tampa and doing local radio. The hardest thing I ever had to do was give up my life on the beach in order to go to Seattle and continue chasing my dream of being the pioneering First Woman. In Tampa, I was able to pick oranges off the tree in my backyard, spend all day on my boat, then come in and take a shower for work at one in the afternoon.

By 7:30 that night, I'd be back on the boat, sipping the orange juice I'd squeezed from my tree that morning. It was a wonderful lifestyle, but I wanted and needed something more in my soul. **What up wit' dat?**

There was something deep in my soul that said I had to break this barrier of being the first. Someone had to do it, and I knew I was the only woman on the scene who had the strength and sense of self and humor to survive what was sure to be a hideous ordeal. **Then as now I always proved that I knew how to do a sports talk show better than anyone.** My secret has always been to be generous with the microphone and never be wrong with my facts and opinions. That I became the reigning maestro of this medium is no coincidence or stroke of good luck: It's been a conscious and concerted effort by me to do whatever was necessary to reach my goal. And don't bullshit yourselves, girls and boys, there is always a price to pay for dreams like mine. I gave up a lot in my personal life—and a lot of what's inside me—in order to knock down this barrier.

This life I've chosen for myself has meant that I've had to go wherever and whenever there might be a chance to move up the radio ladder. Life can be good or life can suck, I learned early, but in my case life always meant moving on to a new town. I saw early on that I couldn't maintain intense personal relationships and move around the way I did. I didn't necessarily like it, but it was my own choice.

Despite apparently having no life outside of the Babe, I do pretty well. Now, everybody I'm close to are people who I've known for ten or twenty years—previous lifetimes in the radioworld years. For the first time in my life, I feel as if I have plenty of old friends, and I no longer even seek out anybody new on a personal level.

There is so little time, I've always felt, and so much to accomplish. Maybe that's why I have made a lot of personal sacrifices so I could inject this natural passion into my work.

So you think the life of the Fabulous Sports Babe sounds glamorous, huh? *Living up in the woods of Petticoat Junction* **WITH NOBODY BUT SPORTSBOY FOR COMPANY?** Do you assholes know what I actually do when I come home from the radio show? I watch "The Simpsons." So no, you idiots, the Sports Babe does not lead a Madonna lifestyle. **The Babe suffers so you might be amused!**

Yet suffer I must, I said to myself, because I have a Higher Cause. By 1989 I knew my global mission was to conquer the airwaves by any means necessary. I also was aware that it was going to be me or nobody to cross the gender line in sports radio. I always knew they could put another woman on national radio and have her talk sports instead of me. But I was also deathly aware that if that woman wasn't as intense or tough as me, then she simply would not be successful.

It takes someone as thick-skinned as me to put up with all the attendant bullshit of being the first woman to host a national sports talk radio show. ***Failure was impossible for me, because it would set all of us women in the field back for a very long time.***

Now, I'm not such an egotistical asshole that I would dare equate my struggle with anybody else's. But *in my own way,* I truly feel that doing my show on ESPN is somehow akin to those who have fought their battles to break down barriers. I feel alone. It always hurts to be first.

The public just doesn't understand that nobody opens doors for you up here in the big leagues because you're a woman. If anything, everyone is trying to slam the door back on you. They don't want you to be here, and they don't want you to do the things you do because you operate so differently.

Women are not what the people who control everything are used to. We just aren't *them,* and they don't understand why anyone with tits would want to come into their little world that they've always controlled so well. The end result is that to be taken seriously you have to work and produce twice as much. It's true, chillun.

And it's not just me. Take **Suzyn Waldman,** who this year became the first woman to ever be a member of a major league baseball broadcast team when she broadcast for the Yankees. Do you think anybody opened any doors for Suzyn? PULL THE THUMBS OUT OF YOUR ASSES, BOYS, **the answer is no.** And what she has done in bringing down those barriers built by those who think no woman can do play-by-play and analysis is monumental.

Now some of you clever pea-brains out there might be wondering about this **"Babe"** business. How, you may wonder, can I self-righteously call myself a feminist pioneer when my name evokes images of the **stupidest twinkie this side of Vanna White?** I will describe in detail later in this chapter the birth of Babe on the radio, but first I will address myself to you dopes who can't see the name is half irony, half a matter of taking the power back.

As far back as 1978 I was practicing what linguists and students of **BABE-OLOGY** have now determined to be the exact measure of informed opinion and witty sarcasm that defines my genius. Still, my act wasn't fully formed until one fateful day in Tampa a decade later when I was broadcasting from my bedroom after a back injury. Out of nowhere, I promised the world they could "spend the day in bed with a fabulous babe." (See page 132.) With that, my recipe for on-air wonderfulness forever became conversational genius mixed with Babe-eautiful attitude—just the mix that today you love so well.

The Babe was more than a shtick, she was me. Within minutes of hearing it, my Tampa audience automatically and forever tagged me "the Babe." The name caused a true furor.

"Oh Babe, OH FABULOUS SPORTS BABE!" the callers to my show would beseech. "You are the queen." When I came back to work after my show at home, there were a bunch of signs welcoming back "the Babe." Someone, meantime, had printed up new business cards for me announcing the presence of the Fabulous Sports Babe.

The phenomenon grew from there into a national movement of the enlightened and the moronic. When I got to Seattle, my new operations manager Rick Scott was adamant that I just use the name Fabulous Sports Babe on-air, and I understood.

I don't hide from the name that was given to me at birth. When people from Tampa phone the show and call me that old name, I don't get pissed, because they knew me when. I do, however, have a problem with people who call me that out-of-date name who never knew me except for my new national radio show. When people call me **"Nancī,"** I feel they are putting me down by not accepting me for who I am as a professional. They put me

down by not realizing I've earned the name of Babe, and justifi-
ably made it my own.

Take the name the oppressors give you and make it your own.
And Babe-aholics have **the Babe.** So if you call my show and
use that other name without a valid reason for doing so, I will
immediately push a button and drop a bomb on your call and your
ass. **I am woman, hear me ROAR.**

The funny part is that the Fabulous Sports Babe and the name
I was formerly known by are truly the same person. A lot of people assume I was never in radio until I invented the Fabulous
Sports Babe eight years ago. Bullshit. I spent a dozen years before
that momentous day in front of the microphone practicing the
routine, which was, in essence, just me. And then one day I was
ready. I hurt my back, and history was about to be made.

I was hitting a bucket of golf balls on a Tuesday morning
when I felt a sudden twinge in my back. What the hell, I figured,
as always the fierce and fearless Babe. So I smacked another
bucket. Somewhere during that second smashing of balls I completely wrecked whatever was left of my once strong and healthy
back. **It was a back that had carried stations and net-
works and more abuse than any** *divine* **woman such
as myself should ever have to suffer.**

Still, the show must go on, so I showed up at work that
Wednesday and did my program even though I was in horrific
pain. By Friday, I could barely move.

On Sunday, I called my cousin and told her that I could no
longer move my legs. I was paralyzed, I told her, and couldn't even
maneuver my own magnificence out of bed. **MY ENTIRE
LIFE FLASHED BEFORE MY EYES.**

An ambulance came to my house and took me away. I was
quickly entombed in the hospital, where handsome young doctors
determined that I had torn a large hunk of ligaments in my back.
The swelling had pushed against my spinal cord, making it impossible for me to either walk or expound pain-free about the idiots
running professional sports.

They pumped me full of Demerol for several days, and as I
floated in a haze, I realized that this shit was clogging my brain,
the only organ that still seemed to be functioning normally. So I

got off the junk and learned that the only thing that would help my unfortunate condition was to lie as flat as Twiggy in bed.

So for a week I lay in my own private hell wondering if I had any chance of salvaging my now apparently shot career. I called work and told them that I was OK, except for the small thing—I couldn't move anymore.

But I could talk, I told the boss, and to prove my point, I yammered so loud and so long at them that they agreed to try and let me broadcast from my hospital room. They didn't really have a choice: Through sheer force of will I prevailed upon them to let me go on-air amid the **clattering soundscape of falling bedpans.**

I needed to get back on, because in this business you are only as good as your last show, and I had been gone for so long in the radio-world scheme of things—a couple of days—that I felt no more relevant than **Barry Manilow.** So the station gofers dutifully showed up in the station van and set up all the necessary satellite dishes and the two-way telecommunications hookups.

All right, so technically a hospital is not a place where a paralyzed patient should set up shop as the most outspoken sports radio expert since the days when football players still had leather earflaps. **But I did it, DAMNIT,** AND DID IT TOUGH AND WITHOUT COMPLAINTS, **the way Knute Rockne would have wanted it.** I did the show for five days from that sick house, and during that time, both my station's ratings and the hospital's rates soared to new untold heights.

After a week, I could no longer bear broadcasting from that asylum. Once, my engineer mistakenly plugged a catheter into the soundboard and suddenly my phone guest disappeared into the ether. There was no way I could survive yet in our station's studio, so the obvious answer as to where to broadcast next was my bedroom. The station set up the computer we used on the show right next to the bed, the satellite dishes went up outside, and my neighbors cheered the daily appearance of the broadcast van.

I broadcast like that for three weeks, lying in bed in a Velcro girdle, making the Airstream jump. And then one day, something came into my brain and out of my mouth. I've said it earlier, but the phrase still sings so nicely that I'd like to hear it again.

"SPEND THE DAY IN BED **with a fabulous babe,**" I told my listeners that day. *HOO-WAH!*

I WAS SHE, AND SHE WAS ME, goo goo ga chew. WE WERE BOTH **the Fabulous Sports Babe.** And yet no matter how many times I explain it, I still get **shit** from people who think my name is sexist. For the last time, all I can say to those who question my judgment is to please go fuck yourselves. Everyone I've ever met who thought it was wrong for me to call myself "Babe" has been unbelievably condescending. What do they care what I call myself?

I named myself Babe, nobody else tagged me with that moniker. By doing so I gave the power of defining myself back to myself—**a power, needless to say, that is forever denied women in most every field between sports broadcasting and chemical engineering.** I'm not a soapbox orator, but I do make my own rules, and I really don't give a shit what the politically correct think of my handle. After all, **it's my handle.**

It all just came together in a magical form in Tampa. I had been doing this afternoon drive-time sports talk show for a couple of years, and all was hunky-dory. Then the station was sold, which happens every couple seconds in this business, and I was asked by the new management to leave quietly through the back door. After the dust cleared, I was promised, I'd get my cash payoff that was customary for talent on the way out in this buccaneering business.

No way, I said, I want my money right now or I'm calling up every newspaper in town and exposing what hideous bloodsuckers you are. I came in the front door, I told them, and that's how I'm leaving. It's been a policy I've long adopted to ensure that I could escape with whatever shard of pride and self-esteem I might have left after being dumped by the latest radio greed-heads in my life. **They paid up. HOO-WAH!**

I was soon hired by a new Tampa station that played country-western music, never a beloved format of the Babe. My charge was to remake the place as an all-sports station. I was given broad powers and little money to accomplish this: I had to strong-arm friends in the business to make free bumpers and liners that we

With all my Babe charm, I helped Lori Keegan, owner of Anna's Ravioli, make her restaurant the "in" place in all of Tampa Bay. Now I get to eat there for free!

could use on the air. I was *Lord Babe,* and though I broadcast from a badly lit broom closet in the middle of nowhere, I'm glad I took the gig. I went out and hired everyone I ever wanted to work with, and the station did all right.

Throughout my career, I've been happy to see, women have been some of my most ardent supporters. After only a week in Seattle, I was already turning the town on its ear. The *Seattle Times* sports editor—a woman named Kathy Henkle—ordered a reporter down to the station to check me out. All Kathy knew was that there was this new woman in town named the Fabulous Sports Babe in a completely male-dominated profession.

Kathy had her profound doubts. As far as she could see, the station had thrown some bimbo onto the air and called her the Fabulous Sports Babe like she was some piece of meat. Before she found out what time it was, Kathy later told me, she thought I was setting the women's movement back twenty years. She thought what I was calling myself was just horrible.

So she sends some reporter over to the studio to rip apart this idiotic new radio voice in town. The scribe duly comes down with his knives sharpened, but I set him straight in about ten minutes. When he got back to the newspaper, he told Kathy he wouldn't be writing a hatchet job after all. "You're going to love this woman," he told his boss—and he was right. Kathy Henkle saw the big picture, and to this day I respect her as one fighting the same battles in a different medium.

THERE ARE ENEMIES TO THE MOVEMENT, sisters, but it ain't me. And I'm not minimizing the sexism that's pandemic in sports. You can see it anywhere, even in commercials that don't even feature women.

There's that commercial, for example, showing some guys in Philadelphia Eagles clothing sneaking out of their dormitory by sliding down bedsheets. The coach interrupts them with a big fat sneer, saying, **"Going somewhere, ladies?"** Funny, I always remember the word "ladies" being a nice, positive thing. In the mouths of some jocks, it's just naturally uttered like a slur.

I'm not put down that much anymore, because I'm the Fabulous Sports Babe, a celebrity more famous than most of the people on my show. But I am not afraid to publicly put some asshole down who is not treating me with respect. If someone's condescending to me, I usually just blow them off. But sometimes I can't help getting nasty. One of my classic to-dos involved this dick Gene Orza, who was Don Fehr's butt-boy in the baseball players' union. He came on the show during the baseball strike, and I said, **"This can't happen! You guys can't go on strike!"**

Well, he was just a patronizing jerk, and I told him that the fans deserved to know what the hell was really going on in the so-called national pastime. Orza then says that the issues involved are too complicated for fans to understand—they're just not smart enough. SO I JUST RIPPED INTO THIS SCHMUCK **like I was Orca** AND HE WAS TASTY **chum**. Then he started to get nasty with me, and I said, "I'm not talking to you anymore," and put the bastard on hold and broke for commercials.

He called ESPN to complain about me, but I stood my ground because he is just a **self-serving asshole prick. His boss Don Fehr, meantime, is an even bigger self-serving**

asshole prick who also believes that fans are too stupid to understand anything related to the business of the game. Of course, Don Fehr never points out that the only person who benefits by labor strife is Don Fehr. If there weren't work stoppages, his like wouldn't have jobs.

Believe me, if Don Fehr had not been involved, the baseball strike would never have happened. Does it really matter, Donnie, if a player is making $2.9 or $3.1 million a year? Why does it matter, Donnie? So a player can walk down the street saying he has the biggest dick in town because he makes a hundred grand more than his teammate? **Well excuse the FUCK out of me.**

This union shit, needless to say, cuts across all sports. Once I had Charles Smith of the New York Knicks on, and I happened to call him the team's union player rep. He gets all haughty and says, "I'm not the player rep, I'm the vice president of the NBA Players Association."

Fine, I'm impressed, mister. I'm pretty friendly with athletes; I ask the tough questions, but I'm not out to hammer them. This guy was such an idiot, though, that I had no alternative but to cut him short most, shall we say, definitively.

Other athletes have no particular ax to grind; they just don't like coming on to talk to a woman who knows more about sports than they do. So they appear as guests and give me tons of attitude, and I'm thinking, If you don't want to give your side of the story, why the hell do you come on in the first place? And then the gloves are off. If you put me down, I will dig you an even deeper ditch to sleep in. **Don't fuck with the Babe.**

Because of these battles I'm forever fighting against stereotypes, I refuse to contemplate the charge of sexism that politically correct nitwits lay at the Babe's welcome mat. No matter what they say, the Fabulous Sports Babe is a **frontier-style feminist.** It is a name I have earned. I *am* the Fabulous Sports Babe, the name by which you know me on ESPN Radio, ESPN2, and in downtown Petticoat Junction. It took me to the top, and if you don't like it, well gee, I'm awfully sorry.

I suppose many of my dim-bulbed but well-meaning fans think it was all ice cream sundaes once I got to ESPN. Wrong. Yes, it's true I'm not only the sole woman to ever have her own national sports talk radio show, I'm also the most famous radio sports talk show host ever. As such, I am constantly trashed by people with **little dinky SPORTS TALK SHOWS** of their own. I have only one question for all these assholes. ESPN had their chance—how come they called me and not you?

What up wit' dat?

There's an enormous amount of professional jealousy in my business—surprise, huh? When I was at Super Bowl XXX, I saw a lot of people whom I used to work with and supported in their careers. Several couldn't repress their jealousy of me. They, of course, were still doing the same things with sports radio in 1996 as they were in 1986. They still just didn't get it. Their idea of sports radio is still verbiage to jerk off to. Their witty repartee consists of **"I like this kind of pizza, and hey, look at the hooters on that one!"**

These, of course, are the clowns trashing me on their own shows. Enjoy those little shows, boys, on those shitty radio stations in those **jerkwater towns** you'll never escape from. Somewhere down in their corroded souls, they know why I'm here and they're there—I'M THE HARDEST-WORKING WOMAN

IN SHOW BUSINESS. ESPN pays me so much because I have an energy level that very few people on the planet can keep up with. That's it. That's the secret.

I sensed when I began at ESPN in 1994 that there were forces at the company that had been brave enough to hire me who were not feeling so fabulous that the Fabulous Sports Babe had been granted a throne. It is a jealous business, what the hey.

Some of these doubters were on-air talent at ESPN who believed that they should have been given four hours a day of national radio exposure, not me. Others who wanted me to drown were behind-the-scenes production people who had friends at other stations whom they thought should have gotten my job.

IT WAS ALWAYS A GUY, A GUY, **a guy giving me headaches.** Some Goober in a suit with a big attitude would be in the studio every day telling me this, bitching about that. The first six months I had the ESPN show, every person on the planet seemed to complain about what I was doing and how I was doing it. But I stood my ground and told all the suits to please get out of my airstream. If they hadn't, I swear to Jesus I would have gotten Uzis and sandbagged the radio booth.

They'd wanted to change me, the essential Babe, into something I wasn't. They wanted to turn me into the **Cokie Roberts of sports broadcasting,** a place where the hardest sports news was explained in the most mind-numbing manner possible. I'm not kidding.

The Babe show, I patiently explained to them, was about entertainment, not statistics. In form and content, Her Fabulousness's soapbox is much more like a game show than Dan Rather's evening news. I told them that if they tried to load their Dan Rather values on me, the show would collapse within minutes. **Just what the FUCK is the frequency, anyway?**

And it would have. If I hadn't fought like a crazed wolverine to keep my show the way it was (and is), they would have turned "The Fabulous Sports Babe Show" into just another crappy piece of boy broadcasting. Under their scenario, we'd have had on "The Fabulous Sports Babe Show" a well-considered and sober five-part story on the National Labor Relations Board. The Babe way, of course, is simply to ask why these dipshits in uniforms are walking off the greatest jobs in the world.

When ESPN told me I should be a more sober and serious host, I simply held up my hand and said wait a minute. "We better have a serious talk right now," I said, "because if this is the kind of program you want me to do, you better get someone else. This is not what I do, **I AM NOT LOOKING TO BE Ted Koppel.**

"And another thing," I went on, **thundering like Pavarotti,** "my job," I told the suits, "is not to make you happy. It's to generate revenue for this network. So let's see how the advertising dollars go, and in the meantime, please just leave me alone."

Oh shit—another Goober paid his phone bill!

As expected, with my larger-than-life mouth, the money started pouring into the network. And when that happened, I was finally able to exact my ignoble revenge on those idiotic men in upstairs offices who tried to turn me into something I wasn't.

Because now I was a star. And the first rule of show business is that the star is always right. I wasn't on a star trip, mind you. If anyone even suggests I'm acting like MADONNA, I issue them a none too delicate **slap.** Rather, I used my new candle-power to reinforce the integrity of "The Fabulous Sports Babe Show."

And somebody in the big corner office remembered that radio isn't about playing records, or reporting the news, or telling the scores. **It's about money, and that's all.**

And since my numbers were more fabulous than anyone could have imagined, I was allowed to thrive. And now, the criticism has come full circle and I'm being asked to pen impressive tomes like this that illustrate my profound education and love of the phrase: **HOO-WAH!**

Now everyone is so supportive, everyone loves me so. A lot of people, I know, will never be supportive because I have a strong personality and they don't. They, needless to say, bother me the least.

And then there are the crazies. What I do on the radio is very aggressive, and a lot of listeners who don't get what I'm about become downright violent toward me. At public appearances, I've been pushed, shoved, yelled at, and threatened. You can bet your ass I have security at these affairs.

My scariest encounter happened in Seattle, where I was actually stalked by a listener who couldn't decide if he loved me or wanted to slice me up. He was just an idiot who liked to send me obscene, violent, and insane mail. He wouldn't back off until a friend of mine in the Seattle police department took care of it. The incident had its effect: It was one of the reasons I left Seattle.

Though I want to fight for the right of free speech, I have no desire to die for it. The Babe must remain alive to inspire a new generation of women and men unafraid to say **"blow me"** in the face of unwinnable odds.

$\mathcal{T}en$

Of Indoor Yachting
and Rattlesnake Racing

The Babe Looks at
the Minor Sports

Hi, this is Charlie Steiner from ESPN. And being a fre-
quent guest on "The Fabulous Sports Babe Show," it's fun to
think back on all the wonderful memories I have of the Fabulous
Sports Babe. For instance, there was that time when . . . naah.
Then there was . . . naah. Or how about the time when . . . say,
we're not recording, are we?
—Charlie Steiner on
the Fabulous Sports Babe's
first anniversary show, July 4, 1995

Once upon a time, not long after man learned to walk erect,
there were four true sports. **Baseball** started in the spring and
ended in the fall, **football** started in the fall and ended before
Christmas, and **basketball** and **hockey** took care of the
rest of the winter. There'd be maybe two good boxing matches a
year; throw in a trip with the kiddies to the Ice Capades and there
you had a full and proper sports season.

Once upon a time is right. Blame it all on television, but for
better or worse, we now live in a world in which **synthetic,
ridiculous, AND UTTERLY INSANE SPORTS** invented solely
because they fit on the small screen are actually surviving.

In fact, these make-believe sports are thriving. Virtually anything that looks halfway athletic will now sell to television,
because we're living in a time when a normal satellite dish can pick
up four hundred stations—each of which needs programming. At
each of these stations, somebody will spin the very low ratings

numbers they get, and from there will be able to prove to advertisers that arena football or indoor yachting is a good buy.

Unless you are wired into a satellite of your own, you wouldn't believe how narrowly these channels broadcast. One of my satellite channels is something called Outdoor Life, which features, I kid you not, programs about nothing but people hiking through streams. That's it. That's the whole channel. But still, this station gets sponsors you wouldn't believe.

Indeed, maybe it makes sense that suddenly the Eddie Bauer company, the outdoor-wear company Patagonia, and fishing gear companies are all interested in buying time on a show detailing how people walk through streams. You can bet there is **serious dough** being generated by these shows, because numbers spinners are now able to prove to advertisers that there's money in bullshit.

The only thing salespeople at some obscure channel need to show advertisers is that their station is **NUMBER ONE with one-armed ladies who live on the left side of their streets.** With just that, they are able to sell the world. For when there is an identifiable market for Speedvision, a satellite channel that runs nothing but old footage of ancient car races, there is a market for everything.

Not that I have any use for modern auto racing either. I mean, what is the fucking point of this sport? Besides wasting immense amounts of money, what is so fascinating about a contest that entails rednecks inside rocket ships on wheels going endlessly around a confined circle? **What up wit' dat?**

I'm firmly convinced the majority of people who go to auto races attend simply because they want to **get drunk** AND SEE A BIG MAJOR CRASH **where human beings die.** I can't imagine any other reason people would go to such bullshit events than the thirst for mayhem.

And that redneck shit that is such a part of auto racing's image? Have you ever gone to one of those races and tried to find anybody with a full set of teeth? You could spend the whole day looking and still not find any. What the hell is that?

Danny Sullivan and Mauricio Gugelmin love me—they've even got Babe stickers on their cars!

Gasp, you may say, isn't the Fabulous Sports Babe afraid of offending militant car racing enthusiasts who listen to my show? Who cares, I say. Auto racing is a very regional sport, which means it just doesn't matter to me. True, if tomorrow on my show I said we were going to talk NASCAR racing, the phone banks would be lit for four hours with racing fans. The same thing would happen if we had an all-bowling show—the lines would be swamped. But the fact is that these are not the listeners I'm looking for; these **gear heads** are maybe 2 percent of our audience. I'm broadcasting "The Fabulous Sports Babe Show" for the other 98 percent of our listeners who live on planet earth and don't believe it's OK to marry your first cousin.

Babe Flashback

On May 31, 1912, Joe Dawson won the second Indianapolis 500 in six hours, forty-two minutes.

Ralph Mulford, meanwhile, was told he had to complete the race for the tenth-place money. It takes him eight hours, fifty-three minutes, as he makes several stops for fried chicken . . . and the finishing rule is changed the next year.

And in case you didn't know it, Mulford was asked after the race whether eating chicken in the car affected his performance. His response: "The breasts got in the way of my driving."

I'm so big that I can afford to piss off the likes of auto racing fans. My numbers are so large right now that I have no need to try and lure to my show the fanatic **NASCAR** or **bowling fan.** I'm so popular that I've gone beyond scrambling for listeners from other talk radio shows, and am now going after

people who listen to rock and roll. The new listener I want is the person punching around the dial looking for music, and is instead amused by me.

If I can get that listener to sit and laugh, I will have conquered the world. This is why I am so hip: I share my listeners with FM rock stations, not talk radio stations whose audiences are mostly old geezers in prison. The Babe, as it were, has no need to "spin" her numbers: She is an intergalactic success.

Not every "sport" has had salesmen as nimble at spinning their numbers for television as car racing or hiking. Among the most obvious losers is **WOMEN'S PROFESSIONAL GOLF,** a sport that has long been considered the ugly stepsister of the men's supposedly more glamorous tour.

This is too bad for many reasons, prime among them being that amateur women and men golfers can learn much more by watching the ladies' tour than their masculine competitors. How many men, for instance, can actually hit like John Daly? But the women's game, with its emphasis on irons and the short game, can be a great study aid for even the best golfers.

I am, I am proud to say both here and on the air, **the world's WORST GOLFER.** But I persevere, and with practice will eventually kick your ass. It's such a peculiar game, and it may just drive me mad.

A few months ago, I was golfing in Orlando. Off the second tee, I somehow found myself trapped in a hellish forest. Wait, I said, I've seen on television how the pros just shoot above the trees and end up where they're supposed to be, far up and centered on the fairway. Sadly, when I hit the ball, it ricocheted off of five trees. I felt like I was stuck in some God-awful pinball machine. What up wit' dat?

Regaining my **Babe-solid** COMPOSURE, I lined up a second shot out of the deep woods. Sadly, I bashed a tree with my five wood, breaking it into three pieces that fit quite nicely into my shoe bag on the trip home. Golf is **Satan's game**—especially if you are a woman trying to make a living at it.

The problem for professional women golfers has historically been that they just don't get nearly enough television coverage. It was very bad for the sport when Dinah Shore died; she alone was able to bring in millions of dollars in advertising support to women's golf with her tournament.

True, there have been some new faces to bring notoriety to the sport. Laura Davis, with her amazingly strong game, has gotten noticed. Then there's Michelle McGann, whom people like to look at because she wears hats or something. But despite having some brand-name recognition, women professional golfers are going to be fucked without that full-time television contract.

As it stands today, a women's LPGA tour event from the middle of last week might be played on tape delay the following Sunday morning at 11 A.M. on Sportschannel. How is a fan ever going to be able to follow a sport that way? But the interest—and the money—just hasn't been there to change or save the sport.

It won't be an easy task for sports like women's golf to catch up to the PGA, its much better endowed stepbrother. It's hard for the women when they're going up against men's sports supported by the people who sell Budweiser and Buicks and tires. **The RIDICULOUS part of this kind of sexism is that *most women drink beer, drive cars, and buy automobile tires.*** But the advertisers have yet to figure out that women make a lot of these supposedly "manly" decisions—or that these women could be easily found in the marketplace watching women's sports. Though the men's side of the tour has money coming out of its ass, it is suffering from an equally dangerous and soul-sapping disease. In a word: **BORING.**

For every **Fuzzy Zoeller** with a buoyant and wonderful personality, there are twenty faceless and nameless guys who'd rather not go for the win, but instead throw the ball up on the green, two-putt, and walk away with a top ten finish. These guys don't have to face all the pressures of a champion, but they still make a fortune. It's not a bad way to make a living.

Insiders in the golf establishment have told me it's good for the game to have ten new and different faces win a tournament each year. Despite our nostalgia for the good old days, these golf guys don't wish us back to the time when **Jack Nicklaus** or **Arnold Palmer** seemed to win nine out of every ten tournaments.

I don't know if I buy this. If that new face in today's PGA tour doesn't win again soon, how will I ever remember him and then cheer him on again? For that matter, can anybody name a golfer who has won two tournaments this year? Beats the hell out of me.

But the final proof of golf's spiritual failure has been the ascension of that **AUSTRALIAN HACK GREG NORMAN.** HE IS THE MOST **OVERHYPED** *thing to come along since Milli Vanilli,* **AND** HE IS ONE OF THE GREATEST PUBLIC RELATIONS SCAMS OF OUR TIMES.

His defenders—can you imagine someone so lame still having defenders?—point out that Greg Norman has won some fifty-odd tournaments. True. But almost all of his victories seem to have been in tournaments with names like the **Botswana Open** and the **Tasmanian Invitational.** To make matters worse, Norman doesn't go to these dipshit tournaments unless he gets half a million dollars up front in appearance fees.

NORMAN, **you Aussie phony!** My big problem with Norman through the 1980s was that he would not play a full schedule on the PGA tour. In my book, if you want to be considered the best golfer in the world, you've got to follow the damn tour.

You cannot be like Greg Norman, telling the world that he can't follow the PGA tour because he is already committed to play the Albanian Pro-Am. I'm sorry, but you can't pick and choose ten weenie tournaments to play in and win. You cannot believe how spirited was the jig I danced when Greg Norman blew his insurmountable lead on the last day of last year's Masters tournament. It was the biggest choke in the history of sports, and it couldn't have happened to a nicer guy. *Thank you, God!* **HOO-WAH!**

Babe's Best Bets

I predict, now that the Baseball Network is dead, the Golf Channel will make a contract pitch to the owners, saying it has plenty of experience dealing with big putts.

Then again, to be fair, I was for once impressed with Norman by the way he handled the loss. His demeanor toward winner Nick Faldo and the media right afterward was commendable in light of what he'd just done.

Then again, **BAD KARMA** follows pretenders like you, Greg Norman, so why don't you just come out and admit that your real job is to sell $500 shoes and $125 hats and $100 polo shirts? Now, I admit that Greg Norman is indeed a pretty good golfer, but he's not as good as a lot of other people on the tour, and he would never have been a big deal if he'd played the tour all the time. But if he is the most colorful human being the professional golf world has to present, then the sport is in even deeper trouble than I had imagined.

Sadly, what has become an even more **monumental bore** than golf is professional tennis. I used to be very interested in the sport, but I can't even remember the last time I actively followed it.

I'm not exactly sure what happened, but now I can watch a set of monumental tennis and feel that what I just saw was as boring as bat shit. I didn't used to feel this way, but that's how I react now whenever I see what's left of the tennis tour.

A big part of the problem, of course, is that **Chris Evert** and **MARTINA NAVRATILOVA** are gone, as are *John McEnroe* and JIMMY CONNERS. True, McEnroe was one of the biggest brats in tennis history, but you couldn't help but watch and enjoy the spectacle that he made. Now all the tennis world has to hold on to in the way of actual human beings with personalities is **Pete Sampras** and **ANDRE AGASSI**. Somehow, the atmosphere around tennis just seems devoid of people you can actually root for.

Babe's Best Bets

I predict Andre Agassi and Brooke Shields will get married, but Brooke will stipulate that Andre has to grow his facial and body hair even longer so the two can appear in a movie called *Creature from the Blue Lagoon*.

Boy, do I wish I could **give a Gillooly** to some of these **spoiled little shits** making their fortunes as tennis players. In behavior, these tennis numbnuts are in direct contrast to the players on the PGA or LPGA tours who, by and large, grew up in a country club atmosphere and somewhere along the line picked up most of the basic social skills.

However, people who are brought up in the tennis world are mostly **OVERINDULGED brats** who have dictated their families' lives and incomes for too many years. They have absolutely no social skills, and as a matter of course are unbelievably rude to people. This directly hurts tennis, because who wants to pay and cheer for some little jerk wearing little white shorts and a terrible attitude?

Women's tennis, especially, is in terrible shape. Look at the **Monica Seles** story. Here's a poor young girl who is stabbed at her place of business, the tennis court. Then it takes her two long and difficult years to recover physically and mentally. So she finally comes back, and within a month is dominating tennis again.

Now what kind of terrible shape is tennis in if Monica can be gone for that long, come back, and still kick everybody's asses? She became the Billy Madison of the tennis world—a grown person who it seemed was performing against kindergartners.

So tennis is just one more sport on the critical list. But it is in no more sad shape than my least favorite sport. **God, I hate soccer. It fills my Babe core with a loathing so deep that it is hard to fathom.** Soccer is a commie sport; no, check that, I don't even consider it a sport at all.

I hate those soccer snobs who like to point out that every six-year-old in the United States plays the game. When those kids turn eighteen, these jerk-offs have been promising for what seems like decades, soccer will completely take over as the most popular American pastime.

Well, frankly, you idiots make me physically ill. I am happy for you that every six-year-old is supposedly playing this ridiculous game. But by the time they're eighteen, these kids won't be playing soccer—they'll be betting on football games. **That's what** time it is in *this* country, **Bubbas. HOO·WAH*!***

Football, of course, remains the king. If American football were introduced in France and Pakistan when those kids were young, they'd be just as crazy over the pigskin as we are.

And, in any case, everybody knows that basketball, not soccer, is the true international sport. Ask children in the Middle East, Japan, and Europe whether they'd rather dribble a ball or kick it into a goal. There would be no contest. Hand me a hoop, you misbegotten soccer fans, and then be so kind as to blow me.

"Oh," I hear you idiots crying, *"the Sports Babe is so unfair. She won't even let us mention our favorite dipshit sports without hanging up on us."*

Need I remind you one more time that it's my show, and if I don't want to talk about soccer I'm not going to? What's the matter with you people? The Babe and her legions of fans want to talk about the big boys, the pro teams of the major sports. Now, of course, when I say "pro teams" I am also including many college football and basketball programs.

So screw arena football AND ALL THE OTHER MADE-UP SPORTING EVENTS **that now clog the airwaves.** Arena football is the worst of the shit: Guys pay a nickel for a team, then pay their players $100 a week. And you know what? They make money—and not a bad amount of money either.

Once again we have to blame television. Specifically, this sad situation has been brought about by the overgrowth in the number of sports channels across the satellite that now find it necessary to bring the likes of porcupine bowling into your home. These stations, no matter how lame, need product. And so we the viewing public get to feast on sports like arena football, rattlesnake racing, and armadillo long jumping. Back in 1982, everybody was making fun of ESPN for BROADCASTING BADMINTON **from Pocatello, Idaho.** But now dozens of sports channels are in the same creaky boat that ESPN was long ago in: How can they get even halfway credible programming?

All of these phony-baloney sports are so poorly choreographed that it makes me ill. I once went to an arena football game and was instantly reminded of watching a made-up event like **"American Gladiators."** The organizers of arena football give fans signs as they enter the stadium gates, and the customers are then instructed to jump around for the grace of the cameras. *What up wit' dat?*

On the surface, all of these bogus sports—and I include in this category the likes of **indoor roller hockey** or **upside-down lacrosse**—are nothing more than obvious crap. Yet somebody is making money. They wouldn't be playing these idiot phony sports unless someone was paying dollars to somebody else to televise them. It's a full-court scam, but it works.

What doesn't work nearly as well as it used to is the marketing of good old red, white, and blue baseball. The sport has put such a bad taste in so many people's mouths these past few years that sometimes I wonder if it will ever come back.

Babe's Best Bets

I predict, now that Cal Ripken is about to tie Lou Gehrig's record for most consecutive games played, he'll focus all his efforts on getting brother Billy to play in two straight major league games.

Personally, I used to be really crazy for baseball. I still like the game, but I no longer consider myself a worshiper at the shrine of baseball. It's simply no longer my highest priority in sports.

Before we begin dissecting the carcass of major league baseball, let us first consider what is right in the game. As always, the game itself is the best part of baseball. Even if you hate the idiots destroying what used to be our national pastime, you can still be thrilled by the white lines on the ball field, the smell of the grass, and the color of the dirt.

For me, there still is no thrill greater in sports than those first moments when you walk into **FENWAY PARK.** You first stroll down a cement walk, away from the gates. Suddenly, you notice your hearing is different—you can now pick up the sound of

Cracker Jacks being crunched and programs being riffled 100 yards away.

You then see the stadium lights, and go through the turnstile. Then you walk up toward the light, and you are soon hit by the sight of absolutely perfect green. The dirt is a beautiful rust color, and then you see the Green Monster and the Citgo sign. **HOO-WAH!**

There's nothing in the entire world like the feelings stirred up by the beautiful sights of Fenway Park. And while I can get bored at any baseball game anytime, it is impossible for me to be bored at Fenway Park. Even if I'm not in the mood to enjoy the pace of another ho-hum, boring-ass baseball game, Fenway Park will always keep me interested.

So baseball is not irretrievably lost, at least for me. No matter what you think of the assholes running or playing major league baseball, you can still get yourself off on the intricacies of the game, the look of sweat and sunshine, or the fact that here is an athletic contest where people who weigh 160 pounds can play against people who weigh 230. **Baseball, AS ALWAYS,** IS THE GREAT **physical equalizer.**

Baseball's majesty came back to me most strongly during the 1995 playoffs. At the time, I'd felt nothing but "fuck you" to all of baseball because the previous season had been canceled by those inconsiderate assholes. And then, to make things farcically worse, they had those numbnut replacement players who came in and tarnished the game even more. Good-bye baseball, I thought, forevermore.

But then came those playoffs, with teams like the Indians and Mariners, and I was right there. God, it was exciting to see Seattle in the thick of a pennant race.

One of the main reasons I got a satellite dish to sit outside my trailer in the first place was to pick up late Mariners games that year. I had lived in Seattle with those sad-ass Mariners when they won only sixty-four games all year, and now I was going to enjoy.

I was there when RANDY JOHNSON decided to switch his number from 51 to 15 in a vain attempt to reverse the team's fortunes. I was also there in the clubhouse when Randy Johnson spent the entire day under his Walkman listening to Iron Butterfly because he thought it would make him a better pitcher. So, of course, he goes out that night to pitch and hits everything in the stadium but the plate.

The Mariner Moose, the team's mascot, was running to get away from Randy's errant tosses, while people sitting in the third row behind the plate were moving seats because they thought they were going to get killed. Those were crazy times in Seattle,

Me and the Big Unit.

but it almost made all the pain and suffering over the years worth it to finally see the Mariners and **Ken Griffey Jr.** go far.

Those playoffs proved to me that I could still get excited by the game of baseball itself. Still, that's a change from what it used to be, when the ballplayers were the personalities that used to bring you out to the ballpark. Now, it's no hot scoop that some of these asshole baseball players are the very reason why people stay home and watch arena football.

It used to be that when people complained about baseball, they'd say things like *"The games take too long"* or *"It's too tedious."* Now they say, **"I don't want to give my money to those asshole owners who are paying idiot ballplayers $5 million a year not to sign autographs."** It's the personalities sending people away from the game.

At the moment, MARGE SCHOTT, owner of the Cincinnati Reds, probably ranks as the most loathed personality in baseball. Marge, of course, is the woman who counts among her top three vices, in no particular order, ALCOHOL, TOBACCO, **and a fondness for Adolf Hitler.**

Now before I say anything in Marge Schott's defense, I want to make clear that I condone none of the idiotic racist or anti-Semitic statements she's made. I was disgusted when she made repeated "nigger" references, but at the same time I'm absolutely sure she's not the only one in baseball who talks that way.

Marge comes from another era, and after she was given the Reds she ran it like the automobile agency her late husband used to run. She operated the team in the kind of old-fashioned way people used to operate a mom-and-pop grocery store. Marge would rather keep prices down for the average Joe coming to a game than win a pennant. In a lot of ways it's worked: The Reds still have the lowest hot dog, parking, and ticket prices in the league. Marge would just rather do it this way on the cheap than go out and purchase a winning team.

Perhaps I don't think Marge is as bad as some people think she is because of an act of kindness she did last year for my assistant Kim Buckley. Appearing on the show one day, Marge mentioned to me that she helps her players who are having problems having a

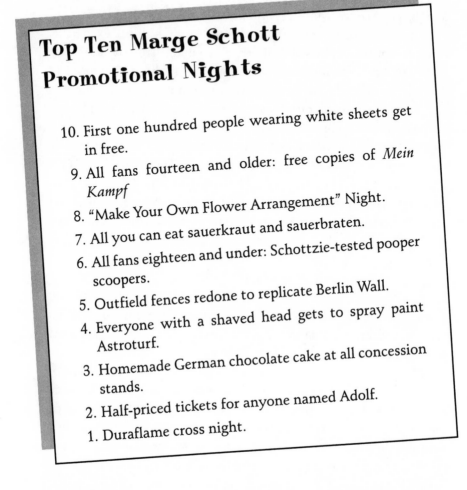

Top Ten Marge Schott Promotional Nights

10. First one hundred people wearing white sheets get in free.
9. All fans fourteen and older: free copies of *Mein Kampf*
8. "Make Your Own Flower Arrangement" Night.
7. All you can eat sauerkraut and sauerbraten.
6. All fans eighteen and under: Schottzie-tested pooper scoopers.
5. Outfield fences redone to replicate Berlin Wall.
4. Everyone with a shaved head gets to spray paint Astroturf.
3. Homemade German chocolate cake at all concession stands.
2. Half-priced tickets for anyone named Adolf.
1. Duraflame cross night.

child by giving them hair from her dead dog Schottzie I. The players are duly informed to put the hair, enclosed in a Baggie, under their mattresses. Invariably, Marge said, their wives get pregnant.

After the show, my assistant Kim was talking to Marge off the air and happened to mention that she and her husband had been trying to have a baby for seven years. A week later, a box showed up at the ESPN studio postmarked Cincinnati. Inside the box was a bag of dog hair and a letter from Marge saying the gift had indeed come from her infamous late Schottzie. The dog hair, Marge went on, would bring Kim luck in having a baby if she only put it under her bed.

Babe's Best Bets

I predict Marge Schott will announce today that the Reds are moving to a new stadium that will test a new type of turf that includes grass and the remaining hair from Schottzie called "Hound Ground."

Interesting, I thought. Schottzie, everybody knew, was dead. What did Marge do—send Cincinnati manager Ray Knight out with a shovel to the pet cemetery to collect the hair? Who knows?

Finally, at the bottom of her letter, Marge had written, **"Us GIRLS HAVE GOT TO stick together."**

Well, I don't know about that, Marge. But Kim did put the hair under her bed and she almost instantaneously ended up getting pregnant with twins and having her babies. Perhaps Shottzie magic had something to do with it. But even if it did, I don't feel a particular bond with Marge just because she's a woman.

Can you believe it? Because of Schottzie, Kim got these two gorgeous babies—Thomas Harry and Kahler Jean.

Still, I understand her situation a little because she, like me, is a woman in a male fraternity that wants her out of the club. The men who run baseball don't want Marge Schott around, and not just because she's not anyone's idea of a brilliant person. **Being an idiot, after all, has never disqualified anyone from owning a major league baseball team.**

After Marge, George Steinbrenner is probably the second most loathed team owner in baseball. Despite his pig-dog reputation, however, I WILL ALWAYS HAVE A CERTAIN **soft spot in my heart for GEORGE,** who is truly one of the most generous guys around. Last year, he even called "The Fabulous Sports Babe Show" on the regular lines and didn't identify himself.

"This is George," he said when Lenny was screening calls. No one knew who he was, so Steinbrenner got put on hold for ten minutes until his turn came up. When he got on the horn with me and identified himself, I said, "George, why didn't you tell them who you were? We could have easily given you the hotline number and you wouldn't have had to wait!"

"I like to be put on hold," George said, "so I can listen."

Now if it sounds like I've come to see the owners' side in the ongoing labor battles with the players' union, you're right. At the very same time, however, I've always seen the players' side. As I have always contended, the players should be paid as much money as they can possibly make because their entire careers can be over in a split microsecond. All I am saying now is that there has to be some sort of a balance.

I don't envy the people in baseball who are supposed to be working this hideous situation out. Take **BUD SELIG,** the acting commissioner of baseball and owner of the Milwaukee Brewers. Known in some circles as **"BUD LIGHT"** for his apparent lack of wisdom or style, Selig is actually quite a lot more interesting than his background as a car salesman would indicate.

I've hammered him, to be sure, on my show. Still, the more I've dealt with Bud Selig, the more I see him as a decent and honorable man. I truly believe he wants to iron out the union negotiations, but he thinks he has to hold fast and tough because baseball is in such a disastrous state.

But God, the first time Bud walked into the studio I thought I was either going to bust a gut or get shot. Bud is a tall guy, and he comes in to ESPN that day with two men who are even bigger.

All three were wearing heavy topcoats, and together they looked like Frank Nitti and his gangster henchmen dressed to shoot up the place for the Chicago **mob**. Bud lightened up considerably on the air, and proved an interesting guest. So now I listen when he says the players are greedy. I also know that the owners are just as greedy. I'm not sure if it's possible, but I hope Bud can find a way clear for everybody.

What I do know is that Bud Selig is always available and candid when you call him at his office. He's the kind of man who has walked across the street at lunchtime for the last twenty-five years and always ordered a hot dog and shot the breeze with the same vendor. *There is something to be said for that kind of man.*

There is no flash or pose or hype to the man, which makes him both a stand-up guy and perhaps the wrong man to save baseball from the show business bullshit of roller hockey and football on ice. **But c'mon, Bud—try.**

Eleven

A Meditation on the Ninth Ring of Hell, and Its Relation to Being a Red Sox Fan, or How I Turned the Curse of the Bambino into the Kiss of the Babe-ino

Hi, this is Lenny the Phone Freak! My favorite memory of the Fabulous Sports Babe occurred last Christmas Eve. It was a cold, windy, and snowy night, and I hadn't seen my family in six months. The Babe, thankfully, had given me permission to see them—as long as I finished my chores around her trailer home.

My family, meantime, is driving the last miles to see me. They've gone through several states and mountains in our 1963 Impala, and I'm scrubbing the Babe's kitchen floor as fast as I can.

And the Babe says, God bless her, I'll never forget this moment, "Phone Freak, as soon as you're done scrubbing, make the bed and start on the bathroom floor. But don't worry about taking out the trash—I'll do it on the way to the Christmas Ball."

—Lenny the Phone Freak, as heard on the Fabulous Sports Babe's first anniversary show, July 4, 1995

Yes, as Lenny's beautiful story attests, the Fabulous Sports Babe is a sentimentalist. In fact, the Babe, as loyal listeners who haven't had their frontal lobes removed are well aware, is so sentimental about one sports town that it counts virtually as her

Achilles' heel. Despite her ice-cool objectivity and sensible cyni-
cism in all matters regarding sports, there is a special private place
where I can be hurt. *In a word:* **Boston.** *In several
more words:* **the Red Sox, Bruins, Celtics,** *and
sometimes* **Patriots.**

It's a classic codependent relationship between the Babe and
her teams. I love them to death, and they keep breaking my heart.
I love my Boston teams and I hate them. The Babe is a woman
who loves too much!

I consider worshiping Boston teams my **religion.** And
like all sects, you have to be a member of the religion before you
are allowed to bash cult heroes. However, no one else can. Don't
you dare come up to the Babe and disrespect the Bosox' Bill
Buckner just because he single-handedly lost the World Series in
1986 to the New York Mets.

However, if you should ask me what I, as a Red Sox fan,
thought of Mr. Buckner, I would tell you he was responsible for
the worst moment of my life. I would go on to call Billy a rotten
cocksucker who I hope dies a million times for letting the ball go
through his hurtin' legs that night, the crippled son of a bitch.
**Ten years later, AND I STILL WANT TO KILL
HIM.** In my mind, the man cannot suffer enough. I will never
forgive him, the prick. No one from Boston has forgiven him
except ESPN's own Peter Gammons, and I even wonder if deep
down in Peter's heart he still harbors a grudge against that man
who lost the World Series.

But again, if you are not a member of the **Red Sox Nation,** do
not attempt to slag Bill Buckner, or any other of our players, unless
you want to end up limping like, well, Bill Buckner. This religion
business is serious with me to the point that there is only one
sports-related feature I plan on having in my house when I finally
get out of this trailer and settle down.

In Jerusalem, there is the Wailing Wall. In Babe's den, one day,
I will have someone build a replica of the **FENWAY PARK Green
Monster.** That's all I want. I don't have autographed baseballs
or posters or any of that other crap that jock-sniffing media types
always fill their houses with. All I want is that Green Monster.

Of course, much of the tradition of being a Red Sox fan is losing.

Yet Red Sox fans always have hope, even when they know their team is shitty. It's beyond the tradition of sucking like the **Chicago Cubs,** because they have the **White Sox** right across town in case they need a breather. But in Boston, our closest team is the dreaded, hated bastards known as the **New York Yankees.**

Because all of New England lives and dies with the Red Sox, we have a true **Red Sox Nation.** In Chicago, meantime, Cubs fans are pretty much restricted to the north side of town, while Yankees fans go maybe as far north as Albany. But the Red Sox Nation encompasses six states, meaning a fan in Bangor, Maine, can suffer as much as a person in downtown Boston.

Being a member of the Red Sox Nation doesn't always mean being tortured by the team—just usually. To this day, the unsentimental Babe still gets *shimmering shivers down her very sensuous spine* when she remembers one particular night in the summer of 1967, the year of the Red Sox Impossible Dream.

If you recall, the Red Sox had sucked for about forever before 1967. And then, suddenly, they were good. They were in a pennant race. Those members of the Red Sox Nation who were unfortunately dead began revolving in their graves in excitement.

One of my most poignant memories of that year took place one July night at eight o'clock, when the Sox were playing the Yankees. I was staying in Cape Cod that summer, and I remember walking down the main street of town unable to hear any of the music you usually heard pouring out of the restaurants and clubs. Instead, you heard the Red Sox game coming out of radios in every building.

As I hit the residential section of town, all I heard was more Red Sox—every single house had the door open and the game on. The game lasted twenty-one innings, and it seemed like nobody in the whole town turned in early. IT WAS MAGIC. The Babe was moved.

The Babe was moved the other way, however, when I was working at a Cape Cod radio station in 1978, the year **Bucky fucking Dent** of those asshole **Yankees** hit that home run to win the pennant from the Red Sox. I still remember watching Carl Yastrzemski popping out to end the game, then pounding on the arms of my chair screaming, **"No, not like this, not**

like this!" But usually it was just like that, year after year, for my beloved, misbegotten team.

Our losing ways, of course, stem from the day in 1920 when the Sox gave young Babe Ruth to the New York Yankees for a broken toaster and three used fungo bats. That's when the team forever went down the toilet, a happenstance that's gone down in history as *"The Curse of the Bambino."*

We are a cruel tribe, the Red Sox Nation, willing to torture not just obvious boll weevils like Bill Buckner, but also our true heroes. Red Sox fans always had a love/hate thing going with CARL YASTRZEMSKI, mostly because he had the gall to take over for **Ted Williams.**

No matter what he did, Yaz was always compared to Teddy Ballgame. Of course, when Williams was actually playing, most Red Sox fans didn't call him **"Teddy Ballgame,"** but rather **"that selfish douche bag who'd rather walk four times than learn how to play left field."**

But that's how Boston is. We hate you when you're here, love you when you're retired, nominate you for sainthood when you're dead. In the same way that Yaz was compared to Ted Williams, **JIM RICE** was compared to Yaz. True, the comparisons weren't as rough for Rice as they'd been for Yaz when he replaced Williams. Then again, it was utterly brutal for Rice to be a black man playing in Boston in the seventies, a time when issues like race and busing were ripping the heart out of the city. It was hard for Rice, because there were many years when he was the only black person in the entire Red Sox organization.

It's amazing how this whole pathetic situation existed only twenty years ago. But leave it to the Red Sox, the last major league club to sign a black man. It wasn't until many years after the Brooklyn Dodgers signed Jackie Robinson that the Sox finally came up with an African-American deemed fit to wear the hose. After passing on Jackie Robinson, Roy Campanella, and almost two decades worth of superstars who went to other teams, the Sox at last signed . . . **Pumpsie Green!**

Red Sox fans, perhaps learning from the team's owners, have of course learned over the decades how to punish ballplayers, too. Sometimes the results have been humorous and entertaining.

Remember when **Jose Canseco,** then of the Oakland A's, showed up at Fenway Park looking like he had just ingested an off-season's worth of testosterone cocktails? **HOO-WAH!**

"STE-ROIDS! STE-ROIDS!" the ballpark denizens chanted en masse to Jose as he stood in the outfield, flexing his **Arnold-size muscles** at them as if he were **Popeye the Sailor Man.**

Meantime, I think the moment Darryl Strawberry began his swirl down the toilet was in the 1986 World Series when he was taunted by the spooky call of **"DARR-YL! DARR-YL!"** It completely freaked Strawberry out, and in many ways I think he didn't get back on his proper nut for years.

But Red Sox fans are equal opportunity tormentors. Who could forget what they did when their own beloved Wade Boggs was revealed to have had a long-term affair with Margo Adams? **"MAR-GO! MAR-GO!"** the Fenway Fans chanted that season whenever Boggs came to the plate.

For all her **bimbo whorishness,** Margo did in fact provide a public service by revealing many aspects of pro ballplayers that are left out of the sports pages. Posing in *Penthouse* after her affair blew up, Margo detailed, among other things, that:

1: Baseball players refuse to perform oral sex on groupies, saving that service only for their wives. (Margo apparently forgot about Pete Rose, who used to like to tell a riddle about his status as Charlie Hustle. "You know why I get so many women?" he'd say. "Because I always go in head first!" *HOO-WAH!*

2: A particular stunt favored by players is to bring a Baseball Annie back to their hotel rooms and begin having sex with her while their roommates pretend to be sleeping a few feet away. The roommate then pretends to wake up, and the two ballplayers have sex with the Annie at the same time.

3: Boggs's superstitions went way beyond eating chicken before every game; he also demanded final say on what underwear Margo wore. After going four-for-five, he learned Margo had not been wearing panties; for good luck, he then asked her not to wear underwear for the next several months.

(Boggs is not alone in his sexual superstitions. Remember Bo Belinsky, the pitcher/swinger for the old L.A. Angels in the sixties who dated *Ann-Margret, Mamie Van Doren, Tina Louise,* and *Connie Stevens?* In his fourth game ever for the Angels, Bo pitched a no-hitter, then went on to compile a lifetime 28–51 record. He always blamed a Baseball Annie whom he'd slept with the night before his no-hitter for the ruins of his career. "I tried to find her [again] and I never did," Belinsky wrote in his autobiography. "She was my good luck charm. When I lost her I lost all my pitching luck." **Oh pleeeze,** Bo.)

4: Boggs hit .341 when she was in the stands, and .221 when his wife was in attendance. And, most shockingly:

5: Nine out of ten items ballplayers were sent to autograph from fans were actually signed by clubhouse flunkies.

Mar-go! Mar-go!

But frankly, all this dirty talk disgusts me. I'm a civilized woman, and prefer that some, or at least one, of my heroes remain untarnished. Ladies and gentleman—**Bobby Orr!**

Ah, Bobby Orr of the Boston Bruins, my all-time favorite player of anything, anywhere. But I love Bobby Orr for reasons beyond the fact that he was the greatest hockey player of all time **(you're the Great One, Wayne Gretzky, BUT YOU AIN'T THE MAN)**.

Bobby Orr completely remade the game, something Gretzky never came close to doing. When Bobby came into the league in 1966, it was considered a very good year for a defenseman if he scored eight goals and had seven assists for a total of 15 points. But then Bobby arrived, and by 1970 he scored 132 points in one year. He totally revolutionized the game.

A lot of the other players on other teams loathed him for it, jealous bastards, but their bullshit never broke Bobby's dignity. I still remember this game when the Bruins were playing the

Buffalo Sabres, and Bobby was hunched over his stick waiting to take a face-off. Over to the side, some low-life garbage piece-of-shit player for the Sabres began skating over to whack Bobby Orr while he wasn't looking. This nobody was going to dick with the greatest hockey player ever.

At the last moment, Bobby finally looked up and saw this idiot coming. But instead of whacking him himself, Orr simply glanced up to the scoreboard, which now read Bruins 7, Buffalo 2, then over at the guy. Screw you. The point was made not with fists, but with class.

Let me just say this about Bobby Orr. When I was living in Boston, I saw a little of **JOHN HAVLICEK,** and I thought he was great. I also watched **Larry Bird,** and also believed he was fabulous. But I never really had any heroes except for Bobby Orr. I thought he was the finest athlete I ever set eyes upon.

But even for dear old Boston, and for dear old me, *loyalty* has its limits. The reality of modern-day sports has made it virtually impossible to stay in love with a team—or even remember who is still playing for them. Like I ranted about earlier in the book, the way players now move around in their game of who'll-pay-me-the-most-money has watered down the whole notion of a set of professionals who spend most of their careers with the same group of athletes in the same town.

The effect of athletes constantly making pilgrimages for dollars like rich Okies is now finally beginning to hit football. Who can remember what team everybody is on? Even I will say **"Irving Fryar is now a . . . what?"** And all it adds up to is fans who don't give a shit. Let me correct myself on that. *Former* fans who don't give a shit.

But, like I said earlier, part of me believes that the reason Boston fans have suffered so is because of the Babe—Ruth, that is. How could it be that that bastard gets sold to the Yankees in 1920 in order to finance Red Sox owner Harry Frazee's expensive tastes in showgirls, in the ultimate betrayal of Boston's soul that has come to be known as the **Curse of the Bambino?**

This is the reason why we suffer, goes the theory in New England, and I believe that you cannot, in the end, fight negative **KARMA.**

And yet I try, how I try, you bastards. Indeed, I've long gone head-to-head against the bad juju of the Curse of the Bambino by offering the equally powerful KISS OF THE **Babe-ino.** To be granted the **Kiss of the BABE-INO** is to be blessed by all that is good and just in the Universe. It is the force guaranteeing your team will win tomorrow, and you will score the winning touchdown.

The Kiss comes from a higher force—the Babe—and is more precious then plutonium. It is the best good voodoo Boston has to offer. **THE KISS,** of course, is not parochial—you don't even have to be on a Boston team to be the beneficiary. A jock can't apply for the **Kiss of the Babe-ino.** Like the MacArthur Genius Grants, the decision

of who to kiss is made by a secret committee of philosophers. Naturally, the committee is ruled by me.

The *Kiss of the Babe-ino* is most often applied to an athlete about to enter an important competition. Scientific research now indicates that the KISS has resulted in a 94 percent success rate, a number unknown in recorded sports history. And yet one dares risk the world if one ignores the Kissed.

For instance, I have given so many Kiss of the Babe-inos to Ken Griffey Jr. that I've now turned to giving him the **Hug** *of the* **Babe-ino,** an almost never awarded level of intimacy. Junior loves me, as he should, and not just because I was there in Seattle during all those terrible years. The Babe is also his hero because Junior knows that without me and my powerful white magic he'd be batting .210 as a platoon player for the Florida Marlins. **HOO-WAH!**

One of the few others to receive an actual **Hug of the Babe-ino** was Heathcliff Slocumb. I still remember him coming up to me at the All Star game a couple years ago in Arlington, Texas, and telling me how much he loved the Fabulous Sports Babe. Unlike most of the phonies in showbiz, Slocumb actually passed the test I administer to see if people have ever heard of me.

I liked this guy, and just decided to give him the **HUG.** And what does the guy do? Goes out and wins the All Star game, thank you very much.

Ken Griffey Jr. would be nowhere without the Kiss of the Babe-ino! And he knows it! Here he is with me at spring training in 1994.

The third and last sports figure to earn the **Hug of the Babe-ino** was Rudy Tomjanovich, the Houston Rockets basketball coach. It was before the first game of the 1995 NBA finals against Orlando, and the world was predicting that the Magic would crush the Rockets.

Shortly before the game, in an arena runway, I ran across an intensely worried Tomjanovich smoking a cigarette. "Rudy!" I said. He put his arms around me, and I hugged him with all the good energy in the Babe.

Needless to say, the Rockets won in four straight games. SEE YA, ORLANDO MAGIC, **THANK YOU VERY MUCH, Hug of the Babe-ino.**

Usually, those who have profited from the **KISS OF THE BABE-INO** phone in to me immediately after their victories. Even coach Jim Herrick called in at seven A.M. West Coast time to thank me for the Kiss the day after UCLA won the NCAA men's basketball title in 1995. He'd been on the show so many times and had been such a great guest that there wasn't even a question as to whether or not to give him the Kiss the day before the big game.

Or please consider the case of the Dallas Cowboys defensive back Larry Brown, who last year, on the eve of the Super Bowl, was granted the KISS OF THE **Babe-ino.** Well, of course Mr. Brown went on to single-handedly win the Super Bowl. He knows he got those interceptions because of me, and is now properly deferential to my power. Bless you, Larry, I am so powerful that at times even I am surprised by the force.

So sure am I of my power that I'm even willing to confess to extremely rare instances of the **KISS of THE BABE-ino** failing those who have received it. For reasons I never understood, these dirty few took the gas pipe after getting the Kiss.

Perhaps the worst example was Walt Weiss, who came on my show one afternoon when he was a shortstop for the Colorado Rockies. Weiss was

Pucker up!

a good guy, and I willingly gave him the rare benediction and *Kiss*. The next day he went out and made four errors in one game. Sorry, Walt, a temp was working that day in the office.

And last but not least there is the unfortunate Danny Cannell. Two years ago, when Cannell was quarterbacking Florida State, I offered up the **Kiss of the *Babe*-ino** shortly before the big Miami–Florida State game. Sadly, Cannell was sacked eight hundred times and got the **shit** KICKED OUT OF HIM.

Cannell, a sport, agreed to come on my show again. This time, however, I told him to come before a game with an easy opponent like Duke. That way, if he blew it, no one could pin it on me or my magic. He did, they won, and the **KISS** was vindicated. **HOO-WAH!**

So take that, Babe Ruth—mother's magic is more powerful than yours!

Twelve
Get a Job, Get a Haircut, Get a Life, and Other Babe Philosophies

I'll tell you what, you're aggravating the people who are paying the freight. You are pissing off America, you are pissing off baseball fans, and evidently you're pissing off the Babe on this Friday, so get over it! It's time for spring training, it's time for baseball, and I think we've all had enough of this!
—Babe on-air rant during the baseball strike

People always ask me, "Oh Fabulous Sports Babe, how did you persevere during those long lean years before Western civilization came to understand your true and utter genius?" I hung on, I always tell my inquisitors, because this—radio—is what I do and all I do.

Bailing out never crossed my mind during my entire checkered career. Maybe it should have—maybe then I'd have that normal life that I never wanted and never cared about. But not doing radio, not being able to step up to the microphone and make the airwaves shake, never entered my psyche. **Not once did I ever even think of giving up.**

Not even when I got fired, which was not rare, did I think of surrendering. All I ever cared about was landing another gig. So I'd hustle and hassle and always somehow manage to get another gig. Somehow I'd manage to continue my quest to grow as an artist, radio personality, and **Nobel Prize–winning chemist.**

It wasn't always easy, to put it mildly, but I simply saw no alternative to chasing my **BABE-VISION.** Invariably, I would begin work at a new station, learn some more ropes, then sooner or later move on. Again, there is no dishonor in the radio business about getting fired; people who have everyday jobs just don't realize how this life-and-death ritual of the airwaves is part of the normal radio experience.

In radio, unlike in the real world, getting fired is nothing to be ashamed of or embarrassed about. If you give up on the medium, however, you're considered by radio people simply to be one of *them*—the sad sack nine-to-fiver straights who just don't understand the magic, allure, and utter hilarity of performing onstage in radio's theater of the mind.

I'm not putting nine-to-five people down, or anyone laboring through the day in, day out routine that defines the lives of most of the planet's inhabitants. Most people simply can't take the **manic peaks** and **depressing valleys.**

On the other hand, if you stick it out and climb to the top like me, you may one day get to go to the **Super Bowl and World Series for FREE.** That ain't nothing. If you quit, you will never experience the rush of having **Roger Clemens's** limo deliver fried chicken from his Rhode Island restaurant to your radio studio.

He did that. To me. To quote the philosopher Butt-Head, that was cool, **ass munch.**

And finally, if you quit the business, you will never know if you could have become a beloved national landmark, like Mount Rushmore or me. You may have your security in your normal job, but you will never have the chance to be as *fabulous* as the Fabulous Sports Babe.

Of course, you would also miss out on some of the side effects and occupational hazards of being host of a show as fast-paced, unrelenting, intense, and pressure-packed as mine. By the time I walk out of the studio each day after four hours worth of dealing with a never-ending parade of **nitwits** and **GOMERS** shrieking at me over the phone, I have no interest in holding any kind of conversation with any human life-form.

After I'm finished with a show, I simply don't want to talk to anybody, see anybody, or hear anybody's opinion on anything. I speak to an average of two hundred callers a day, which means over a thousand voices are rattling around my brain each week. I am gone. I turn on some opera and close my eyes.

Inside my trailer I've built a veritable nonsports civilization that offers no clues to the fact that the Fabulous Sports Babe lives here. I feel my varied interests inform and improve my show, and make me more well-rounded than 99 percent of the shit-for-brains talk show hosts making their livings sniffing around jocks for stories. **MY FABULOUS ART COLLECTION? My love of the opera and ballet and foreign films?** All these passions of mine come together to help "The Fabulous Sports Babe Show" be the most entertaining and informative program in the entire airstream.

How? Because knowing more about life besides sports means I am not a dipshit. It means I can then take my show past sports in order to discuss bigger topics like bigotry and sexism. Maybe that's why people who aren't even sports fans listen to "The Fabulous Sports Babe Show"—because they know they'll hear more than just conversations that go:

CALLER: You idiot, THEY SHOULD HAVE BROUGHT THE LEFT-HANDER IN IN THE SIXTH!

RADIO HOST: *What the hell do you know!*

I would die if I was restricted to that kind of social intercourse. While sports is my living, it doesn't define my act. It's been good to me, but I don't want to be perceived as some **girl jock WITH HER FEET UP ON THE coffee table** who spends all her time watching just another basketball game.

To be honest, I *will* often watch that basketball game. But I will observe that hoops contest from a different angle than a lot of the world. Watching that game does not define who I am. I'm not the **couch potato** wasting away in front of the tube watching my life flicker away. I'm absorbing what I'm seeing, and making my own critical judgments for the betterment of my show.

But just because I won't cut off my own legs in order to see every game does not imply, you idiots, that the Babe is anything less than utterly informed on the sports of the day. By flipping around the offerings on my satellite dish, I can watch pieces of six games a night in only two or three hours. Even with that, there's still time in my evening to listen to all of *Aïda.*

Then, the next morning before the show, I'll read the sports pages of the *New York Post,* the *New York Times,* the *Boston Globe,* *USA Today,* the *Hartford Courant,* the *Los Angeles Times,* the *Tampa*

Tribune, and the *Atlanta Constitution.* I'll also have sports columns faxed to me from newspapers in Detroit, Chicago, Miami, and San Francisco. All of the assorted news wires come right into my office at ESPN, so I also know, seconds after anything has happened in the sports world, what has occurred—and maybe even why.

Still, once in a while I'll wonder if I'm not slipping into that crazy world that many sportscasters live in where all of life can be reduced to sports. Once in a while, when it's two in the morning and I'm watching some who-cares game on ESPN, I'll call a friend and say, **"Oh Mikey, I need to get a life."**

Only rarely does that happen, and if I weren't such a highly tuned moral force in the universe no one else would detect my fear of having no life outside of the sports world. But always, deep down, I know if I'm losing my perspective on the real world. Luckily, though, **THE FABULOUS SPORTS BABE HAS BEEN BLESSED WITH MUCH self-esteem. I know I am simply fabulous.**

One smart way I've devised to avoid going crazy in this business is to pay no attention to whatever the competition is doing. If you believe in yourself, which is not difficult when you are as divine as I, then there is no need to know what the chipmunks trying to imitate you are up to.

I don't mean you don't share with your competitors: I've always believed all we reporters were in this soup together, and when I worked at local stations I'd always give someone tape or sound bites if they were late or behind.

A lot of other small-timers wouldn't do that to help their competition, but the Babe believes in good karma and the fellowship of radio comrades. Some of them, anyway—**the rest can go to *hell* on the express train.**

In radio, as in life, one needs an accurate and honest *bullshit detector.* I always know if what I'm doing on the air is right, and when I feel that my efforts are hitting the mark, I'm confident no one on Mothership Earth can dethrone me as Queen of the Airwaves. Even when no one else has a clue as to what's going on with the program, I believe that I have a gauge inside me that tells me if I'm doing something right or wrong on the air.

Call it my sixth sense; I prefer the notion of divine omniscience. I can feel what the show lacks before anyone else even notices anything is wrong, or stale, or stupid with the program. Be it a new fake commercial or a fresh cut from the Royal Babe Orchestra, I am the **final and only arbiter** of what is needed and when it should be done. While I will listen to other people's thoughts about the show, no one knows what's good for "The Fabulous Sports Babe Show" better than I do. My staff can put in their two cents about what to do, but if I say no, for any reason, it's positively no. **HOO-WAH!**

It has to be that way on "The Fabulous Sports Babe Show," and I would never work in any other way. It's my show, I tell the people who work with me, and we'll do it exactly the way I like it done. You all can surely help me, I tell my staff.

Once, I got soft and gave Denis the Sportsboy a rare vacation. Before he left, he agreed to train the guy who would be taking his place. During his office orientation, the substitute asked Sportsboy in my presence what he needed to know. Sportsboy then pointed at me, smart idiot that he is, and said, "WHATEVER SHE SAYS IS RIGHT, **and you do it. You are her slave.**"

24-7-365.

Perhaps my most noted philosophical theorem, however, is the oft-repeated, seldom understood notion of *"Get a job,* GET A HAIRCUT, get a life.*"* On one hand, it is a simple command to arrested adolescents to get their noses out of *fantasy baseball and football leagues and grow up.* It's a call to overgrown slackers to get a real job, start looking like a human being, and go to work, for chrissakes.

I'm sure some of you one-track morons who haven't paid attention to my message wonder what gives me the right to judge those who are obsessed with sports to the exclusion of all else going on on the planet. Aren't I the one who must eat, breathe, and live sports in order to stay ahead of the bloodthirsty pack of radio talk show hosts who would love to take a bite out of my **number one-rated ass? HOO-WAH!**

Yes, that's me, you idiots. I'm the hardest-working woman in showbiz. But I'm also a person with a life, even when I'm stranded in sad-ass Petticoat Junction.

Now, I prefer to watch parts of a lot of football games and

leave a few extra hours in which I can actually impersonate a human being. In any case, I am so good at what I do that if I see a piece of every NFL game on Sunday, I can talk knowledgeably about it all the next day on my show. I'm expert at watching multiple games on the tube at once; I learned the feat back in 1980 at WEEI radio in Boston, where I used to have to watch five different televisions at once.

This was before remote controls, so I jerry-rigged them so I could change channels by pulling on a pair of pliers. After that bullshit, surfing my satellite for a piece of some far-flung football game is absolutely no problem.

I still remember the caller last year who asked me on the air, "Did you see this-and-that basketball game last night?" It was some meaningless contest that only utter basketball junkies would have ever cared about, so I told the guy to get a life.

"Now listen," I said, "last night, back to back on television were the films *Babette's Feast* and *Like Water for Chocolate*. Both are Academy Award winners. Now should I watch those two fabulous films or just another basketball game? You can bet it's not basketball showing at my house that night."

So get a life, you assholes! I have many personal antidotes to sports burnout, the prime cure being to get my ass to the opera. I started getting into it way back when I was living on Cape Cod in a garage above an older woman who liked to get crocked every Sunday afternoon and put on Luciano Pavarotti records at top volume. God, she cranked his ass up, and I grew to love the sound of Pavarotti shaking the walls with nothing but his vocal cords.

I learned my opera chops over the years, becoming a huge fan of **Puccini,** especially his opera *Madama Butterfly*. (See Appendix.) I must have seen *Madama Butterfly* a million times, and I challenge any nitwit savants out there to beat my knowledge of the operas *Don Giovanni* and *Carmen*. If my king is **Pavarotti,** my queen is the late, great MARIA CALLAS, the greatest soprano ever. I know who to hate, too—that Nazi bastard Richard Wagner can rise from his circle of hell and blow me. Are you listening, idiots? You're going to be tested on this material.

Perhaps the crowning moment of my career as an opera buff

happened last year, when I finally saw Luciano Pavarotti live at the Metropolitan Opera House in New York. He was performing in *I Pagliacci,* the opera about a beleaguered clown, and Pavarotti's performance was no less important to me than any sporting event I have ever attended. No World Series game ever beat this experience, nor any Super Bowl.

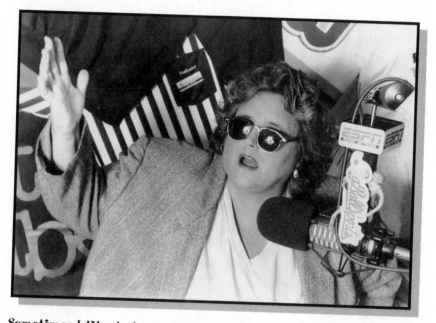

Sometimes I like to turn off the mike and belt a little Puccini in the airstream.

In its way, the Metropolitan Opera is as exciting a place to sit as Fenway Park. I was in the eighth row for *I Pagliacci,* and I couldn't stop staring at the wild-ass chandeliers dangling above. I was like a little kid staring up at these fixtures that looked like Medusa hair made out of spun glass.

And then came the overture, and a wagon drawn by a real horse came out onto the stage. Finally, Pavarotti came out of the wagon and started singing. He filled the room with that voice, and I was absolutely pinned to the back of my seat in wonder. **"HOLY SHIT," I said, "*this is what I've been waiting for* my entire life."**

Don't worry, you fans of mine who think I must have had a stroke to go on this way about something that has nothing to do with earned run averages or yards per carry ratios. Because I *still* react to the opera in the old Fabulous Babe way. I don't become this other person when they start singing *I Pagliacci*. Instead, I'm sitting there singing along like the old commercial that went, **"No more Rice Krispies! We've run out of Rice Krispies!"**

If imminent danger lurks on the stage for one of the characters, I don't start whispering in Italian. Instead, I'll lean over to whomever I'm with and say, *"Oh, look at this, he's about to take the gas pipe."*

I also heed my own call to get a life by not reading the sports pages or watching Sportscenter when I'm on vacation. I used to fret when I went away that if I didn't keep up with every tidbit of sports news I'd miss something important and get burned by some caller who knew more than me.

But I've learned not to be afraid of missing something while I'm on vacation. I did it by finally realizing that the world isn't going to fall apart if I do, and I'll still have my job even if I didn't see the item about the third string Chargers running back who was cut three weeks ago. I didn't used to feel this balanced about my work, but in learning how to have a life, I figured out how necessary it was for me to turn my brain completely off.

It's not just male callers to "The Fabulous Sports Babe Show" who need to heed my decree to **get a job, get a haircut, get a L I F E**. One person especially who should be listening to my sermons on the subject is Rebecca Lobo, the basketball player who led the University of Connecticut to the NCAA Women's championships.

So what is she doing now? She has been off the basketball team for a year, and she's still parading around to luncheons in order to accept awards.

Get a life, Rebecca—there's more to existence than walking around picking up awards. **Jesus Christ, GO TO WORK, girlfriend.** It's not the Fabulous Sports Babe's fault that you decided that the only athletic skills you wanted were ones that were completely unmarketable. If you were going to play a sport when you were growing up, why did you pick girls' basketball, for chrissakes? You should have picked up a golf club or tennis racket. Let's make some money out there, Rebecca!

And though I stand in righteous judgment of any and all such idiots, I have never held myself up to be some sort of supreme arbiter of right and wrong. I hate the pompous nitwits of the sporting press who feel that they are making the world safe for peace, freedom, and the **Minnesota Fighting Pike of the Arena Football League.** I make no pretensions toward being the sports world's answer to **Woodward, Bernstein, OR EVEN Geraldo Rivera.**

I'm in *showbiz*, not journalism, and don't forget it. I still remember this guy from Albany, New York, who called me in all seriousness last year in order to tell me, "This is the very first time I have ever heard your show, and I just want to commend you for everything because the journalistic integrity of your program is so high."

I almost spit out my soup, the only mood-altering compound I allow myself while on the air. I told him, "Honey, wait until Thursday, because that's when we reach our journalistic apex. **That's GEEK-OF-THE-WEEK day, you stupid weenie!** [I love bleeping myself.] Now relax and have some fun, fer chrissakes."

Babe Flashback

On May 9, 1932, Burgoo King won the Preakness. Not many people know that Burgoo King's performance was the inspiration for the hamburger chain that competes with McDonald's. In fact, word has it that Burgoo King was the original whopper.

Journalism my ass. We're putting on a show here, kids, just putting on a show. Obviously it's part of my job to disseminate information, but I can't just sit in my chair and read the wire clippings to my audience. I don't get paid to pretend I'm Diane Sawyer and intone, "This just in from Dallas . . . Frederick Q. Moron was just released on waivers."

That's not a show! But it is a show if that copy comes in about somebody getting cut, and I make a crack about let's give that unfortunate player some lovely parting gifts, including a copy of the home game of the National Football League, like he's some loser on a game show. It is a show if instead of piously saying a player was let go, I say **"He took the gas pipe,"** one of my all-time favorite expressions for going in the tank.

If I don't fool myself about the deeper meaning of what I'm doing, I also don't delude myself into granting my callers any more credit than they deserve. On most talk radio shows, especially self-help programs, the host assumes the person calling is reasonably together and there is something terribly wrong with the person the caller is bitching about.

As I said earlier in the book, however, I go on the assumption that *anybody who calls me is an idiot,* A COMPLETE MORON, **or just plain NUTS.** That way I'm occasionally pleasantly surprised. But this is my show, and I violently disagree with people who think it is their God-given birthright to dial a number and speak with me for as long as they like on the radio.

My answer to these idiots is for them to get their own damn show. As I say to **idiot callers** all the time, "I don't have to listen to you or put you on the air, and if you don't like it you can hang up the phone and change the radio station. But I must be doing something right, because people love that I always hang up on your ass."

You just can't believe how stupid some people are. There are tons of fucking Goobers out there who actually think I'm broadcasting from their town. They're completely oblivious to the fact that this is a national show, and we're not based in Raleigh, or Houston, or Denver. Some of my callers, I'm telling you, must have worked as extras during the filming of *Deliverance*.

All of you, **PLEASE, PLEASE, PLEASE grow a brain.** And then, *please, please, please* **get a life.** If you don't, I will have no choice but to request that you please leave me, *Madame Rolonda*, alone.

Again, I'm talking about callers here, not listeners. Because I am completely convinced that you have to be an utter moron to call up a radio station and chat, right? But to be a listener at the radio shrine of the Fabulous Sports Babe is to be of a substantially higher moral and intellectual order.

For instance, you rarely hear a woman calling my show. If we're lucky, we'll get one a day. But when I take the Babe show on the road for public appearances, half the people who come to see me are women.

They're listeners, or they wouldn't be there to greet me. They don't call because only **testosterone-crazed idiots** seem to feel the compunction to ring a radio program. Hence, it's only been in the last few years that I've come to realize that women who aren't in power in their workplace feel a real kinship with me.

These women feel, they tell me, that they want to hang up on their bosses the way I hang up on my obnoxious callers. They want to talk to their bosses—or someone in their lives—the way I talk to the morons who dial me up on the air. But they can't do it, for whatever reasons, so I do it for them. I had no idea that this kind of listener looking for a vicarious thrill actually existed. But they do, and I'm gratified by their loyalty and devotion to my fabulousness.

These people have lives, or are fighting to have lives, and they have my respect. But those other idiots who call me up with their idiot no-life questions?

So how does one not become a human being who needs to be told to get a job, get a haircut, get a life? As always, the answer is simple. Carpe diem. *"Seize the day,"* **you fucking morons.** I've said it before, and I'll say it again. **CARPE DIEM!**

Seize the day, indeed. In one way or another I preach this lesson every day on "The Fabulous Sports Babe Show." It doesn't matter whether you are a professional athlete or a truck driver. No matter who you are, you have to be able to read the room and seize the soul of each and every day.

Reading a room means being perceptive enough to be able to stand back from a situation and truly understand what is going on right before your face. Reading a room goes far beyond just knowing whose hand to shake—it means knowing what is expected of you and then being able to deliver.

I run my office and staff by the same principles. My crew on "The Fabulous Sports Babe Show" knows they better be able to read the fucking room of my world every day, or they're gone. They must understand that if I don't have their complete loyalty, they will be summarily *banished to the netherworld.*

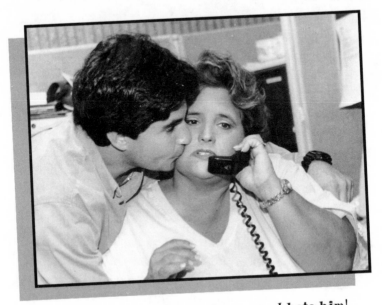

Producer Billy Rodman loves me—I hate him!

Usually, banishment from my queendom for an offending staffer takes the form of a **SPECIAL PENALTY BOX** that exists only in their minds. If someone doesn't read my room right I will have them work every weekend for an entire summer. The crimes they might have committed to be so banished range from outright treachery to the coveting of a job that isn't theirs.

I tell my staff from the beginning that "The Fabulous Sports Babe Show" is not a place to come and learn. There are millions of dollars riding on this show, and I don't want some incompetent and/or in-training person dinking around with how it runs.

So don't come up to me, I tell them all, and say you want to try and screen phone calls. Nobody is more of an asshole in screening calls than **Denis the Sportsboy** or **Lenny the PHONE FREAK,** so let them do it. Why screw up the show with a shitty caller that got through because some neophyte wannabe wanted to learn how to screen phone calls that day?

Read the room, boys and girls, wherever and whatever that room may be.

Timing is everything in life, I tell my listeners and underlings, so don't screw up what may be your one big chance. And forget the notion of being popular. Being liked is not what life is all about.

For instance, it is no secret that I don't give a shit one way or another if some of my callers and audience hate my fabulous guts. I still remember the day some Southern redneck schmuck called and told Sportsboy on

Lenny the Phone Freak with stupid Drew Hayes, ESPN Radio general manager.

the screening line, "I want to talk to the big fat broad."

"HOLD ON," Sportsboy said, *"and I'll get you the phone number of your sister."* Well, the guy went apeshit and began screaming, at which point I got on the line and told the fellow, "Now you're fucked." It was a beautiful moment in radio broadcast history.

Sportsboy also goes out of his way to keep me away from the more noxious faxes that our idiot listeners send to me. He does this not to protect me, but because he knows I will go far out of my way to call these bastards up and destroy them with a "fuck you" or two. These bastards have no life, or why else would they be faxing a sports talk radio show in the middle of a workday? They wouldn't know a good football coach if they were standing in line getting blown by one.

I don't know where these people get the idea that "The Fabulous Sports Babe Show" is a forum for the free exchange of ideas. They have not listened to my lectures concerning exercising their rights to **Babe-ocracy**—a concept that simply means this is my show and they come into the arena at their own risk.

So if I decide that every single caller who ever phones in from Memphis must first do an **ELVIS** impersonation on the air, so be it. If they refuse to honor the King, and I, with an impression, I immediately **blow their asses up**. No matter how much they bitch, they simply must do Elvis. If they continue to complain I simply tell them that this is my show. "You do what I want, you asshole," I tell them.

My publicist Mark Samson—I hate him too!

Naturally, this attitude did not sit well with one of the honchos at our Memphis affiliate. He faxed the show and told us we would be off the air in his market if we didn't make some changes. Change one, he demanded, was for us to stop tormenting his Memphis listeners by making them do Elvis impersonations.

Apparently among the snooties of Memphis, **Elvis** is not considered a local treasure, but a **white-trash embarrassment.** Well, that station manager had his head utterly up his ass. I still make Memphis callers do an impersonation of the King, and we still get heard in Memphis. Go to hell, you bastards who don't get the meaning of a very simple joke.

You just can't believe the idiots we run into on the road. We had a mostly beautiful crowd of Babe believers last year when we were broadcasting from a Detroit sports bar. Lines for my fabulous autograph stretched around the block six deep, and I felt like the **Pope.**

Except, standing in line was some idiot wearing a toupee on his head that looked like some species of dead squirrel. I don't know if he was drunk or just unbelievably stupid, but he kept saying he wasn't going to leave until the **BABE hugged and kissed** him and gave him an autographed picture.

I looked him over and said forget it, **abso-Gillooly** not. He had the look of the kind of jerk-off guy who has a collection of autographed celebrity pictures that he carries around as proof that he knows fame. Indeed, as he's standing there like an idiot, he starts telling us of all the beautiful famous women he's dated and slept with. He simply wouldn't go away.

Nathan, the Junior Sportsboy.

Finally, the largest security guard in the history of security guards comes over and drawls to this idiot, **"She ain't gawna kiss you."** Yeah, you dummy, I chimed in. And then he was gone. And these, my friend, are some of the members of the Babe army.

Of course, not all of my fans and callers are JEFFREY DAHMER TYPES. I still remember last year when I was in Orlando staying at the **Disney Institute,** where I was delivering a lecture on cold fusion. Splitting atoms has always been a fabulous little hobby for the Babe, an avocation that even won me the *Nobel Prize in physics* in 1991.

One morning during my sojourn at the DISNEY INSTITUTE, I availed myself of the think tank's glorious spa. I was in heaven that day, lying there under a seaweed mask with cucumbers on my eyes. As I was being pampered, the relaxing sounds of the New Age were coming out of the cassette deck that my masseuse was controlling. I, wrapped in warm towels in this womblike room, was finally free to let my mind wander and roam. How, I mused, could I save mankind from itself?

Suddenly, three loud knocks on the outside door interrupted my relaxation session. I told the masseuse that maybe we should open the door, but she refused to break our karmic momentum. "We cannot upset the experience," she said.

But the knocking persisted, and finally she went and opened the door, returning with a note. **Michael Eisner,** the message read, would like to meet with me in an hour and a half. Could I make it?

Uh, yeah. Eisner, the head of Disney, had just picked up a nice little bauble in the form of **ABC.** ABC, of course, owns ESPN, so in a sense Eisner was my head don. Yes, I messaged back, I'll somehow find time in my busy schedule to take the meeting.

A few minutes later, my masseuse and I heard the same insistent knocking that we'd heard a few minutes before. It was the messenger again, and this time he wanted to know if I could meet Mike Eisner right now. The Disney, ABC, and ESPN king was downstairs at the moment, I was told, and waiting for my answer. Uh, OK.

Babe's Best Bets

Some predictions on how things will be different at ESPN now that it's going to be owned by Disney.

I predict the minority hiring policy will be expanded to include dwarves, witches, and talking chipmunks.

I predict SportsCenter will feature a nightly parade across the set . . . and I predict every day on the Babe show, a Mighty Duck update.

So I hustle down and meet my new boss. Michael Eisner is a tall drink of water, about 6'4", and he had a henchwoman with him who was wearing this big **MICKEY MOUSE PIN** with ears made out of pearls. Christ, I thought, how long do you have to be with this company to get that little show of appreciation?

The head cheese then sticks out his hand and says, "I'm Mike Eisner."

"And I'm the Fabulous Sports Babe," I retorted.

"I know exactly who you are," he said most reassuringly.

Eisner then told me that he wanted to do a sitcom based on the Fabulous Sports Babe, a notion I rather enjoyed. I said, "So what else is happening, Mikey? Mikey, what else is going on?"

He laughed. No one called him Mikey, but my utter fabulousness conquers all. We talked for about fifteen minutes, and I gave him a Babe T-shirt and an autograph. Yes, he was the most powerful man in show business, but Eisner was just one of the many who come to my altar in the hopes of perhaps touching my hem.

Now, in Michael Eisner we're dealing with a man who most certainly doesn't need to go out and get a life. He's got a *good haircut,* **a bitchin' job, AND HE CARPE DIEMS EVERY GODDAMN DAY OF HIS LIFE.**

If, like Michael Eisner, you heed the Fabulous Sports Babe's philosophy of life, you might just end up running your own multinational corporation. Then again, considering the demographics and IQs of my average listener, maybe not.

The nine-foot Michael Eisner!

A final note on the Olympics . . .

I am still amused when I hear idiot callers talking about professional sports as if they were actually just games. Wise up, Bubbas! Athletics, like the radio business, is solely about Showtime, which of course is just another word for money.

Nowhere was this more evident to me than when I went down to the Olympics in Atlanta. To put it lightly, the scene was a fucking **disaster.** Atlanta was in no way prepared for the number of people who showed up—it simply couldn't move them around town. It was a hideous mess, like being trapped in a Southern version of Calcutta.

Meanwhile, I never saw such price gouging in my life. It cost **$5** for a little six-ounce Coke! Still, it was worth every penny of the six hundred bucks they were charging to see the opening ceremonies. It was one of the most awesome sights I've ever seen.

I'm sure my memories of Atlanta would be fonder if I hadn't wrenched my back early on, forcing me to watch the rest of the Olympics on TV. My memories of the Olympics were skewed by mishap; I'm sure in a year I'll be bragging about what a fabulous time I had at the Games.

For now, though, the most enduring images I've taken from the Olympics are two of gymnast/heroine **KERRI STRUG.** The first scene was right after she smashed her ankle and won the gold, and then told the world in that **Minnie Mouse** voice that her gymnastics career was over and that she was now going to go to college.

Then, five days later, there is brave Kerri on "The Today Show" with her foot propped up as she tells the world that she's just hired the biggest agent on the planet. She'd gone from Minnie Mouse to hiring Leigh Steinberg in mere hours! Two weeks after that, Kerri was in the Babe's Airstream with her foot propped up. She actually thought I was **serious** when I asked her to do a back flip out the door when she was leaving. Gimme a **break!**

ABC's Tom Joyner—this was the only good time I had at the Olympics.

So carpe diem, Kerri, and godspeed, and prop that foot up all the way to the bank. Because you seized the moment, you now have a job, a professional haircut, and an actual life. Now, if only my callers could be so motivated.

But hey, why can't they? Hey, Bubbas, sweep up those pizza crusts, take your feet off the furniture, and throw away those fantasy Baseball magazines. Read another section of the paper besides the sports page. Attend a public event where you can't buy nachos with or without melted Cheez Whiz.

It's never too late to get a life. **CARPE DIEM, ya bastards!**

Fun in the sun. I took over ESPN's new hot spot at Walt Disney World and—of course—turned it into my own personal playground. Welcome to Babeworld!

Top Ten Attractions at Babeworld

10. The Harmless Pittsburgh Pirates of the Caribbean

9. Albert Belle's Tunnel of Love

8. The Spinning Jockey Cups

7. Marge Schott's Hall of Nazi Dictators

6. The Bill Buckner Croquet Course

5. Babeworld map that unfolds into the shape of Dennis Rodman, with tattoo figures of each of the park's attractions

4. The Ken Behring Fun Arcade, featuring grab machines full of miniature, stuffed office secretaries

3. The Michael Irvin Food Court, serving refreshing coke

2. The Belmont Stakes' Stable Boy Heavy Petting Zoo

And the number one attraction at Babeworld . . .

1. O.J.'s House of Horrors!

The Fabulous Sports Babe's
Bravissimo Guide to
Fine Cinema and the Opera

As any asshole who's listened to my program for eleven minutes knows, my four abiding passions, in no particular order, are **PRO FOOTBALL, FILM, THE BOSTON RED SOX,** and *the opera.* Since I've already discussed pro football and Boston in depth, it remains for me to educate you, my legions, as quickly as possible concerning the beauty and mystery of the cinema and opera.

Yet sadly, reality overwhelms me. And anyway, what is reality? As Lily Tomlin so aptly put it, ***reality is nothing more than a collective hunch.*** And my own collective hunch is that my readership has no more interest in the art of Fellini and Pavarotti than they do in playing rock, paper, scissors with Albert Belle.

Very well then. I will adapt my lists of must-see movies to encompass only sports films. But you're still going to get your dose of opera, ya bastards. Don't panic—my tutorials come in a dimwit version, with wisdom prechewed and predigested for idiots who only know the opera house to be the place where it ain't over until the fat lady sings.

If that's what you think, then you are an idiot. Maria Callas, the greatest soprano in the history of sopranos, was also a beauty. In any case, need I remind you in these last 224 pages that this is my book, and goddamnit, I'm determined that you're going to learn something. So herewith my top movies of several different sports, including brilliant critical opinions by the Fabulous Film Babe herself. **HOO-WAH*!***

Let us begin with the top five films of boxing, that most cinematic of sports. Warning: The film *Rocky* will not be mentioned in this list. As always, the Babe is not frightened of voicing unpopular opinions. And if Sly Stallone doesn't like it he can just come kiss my fine ass.

1: ***Raging Bull*** (1980). The greatest boxing film of all time, the best performance ever given by Robert De Niro—the bastard—and the finest film ever directed by that flyweight in poundage only, director Martin Scorsese. The biography of middleweight champion Jake La Motta, the film has the most authentic fight action since Tyson–Givens. Joe Pesci made his debut in this film as La Motta's crazy (surprise!) brother. And Cathy Moriarty as Jake's heavenly wife beats Talia Shire as a ringside gal pal on a first-round TKO. Marty, you made a classic.

2: ***Kid Galahad*** (1937). Abso-Gillooly a fine movie. Edward G. Robinson plays a tough-guy-with-a-heart-of-gold boxing promoter who finds a champ but loses his moll, played by Bette Davis. Humphrey Bogart is in his bad-guy prime as the gangster boxing promoter looking to grind Robinson into tofu. And don't rent the stinker remake of this with Elvis!

3: ***Requiem for a Heavyweight*** (1962). Here is Rod Serling writing at his best, you lunkheads who think he only did "Twilight Zone." Anthony Quinn plays a washed-up fighter hitting the skids. Throw in Jackie Gleason, Mickey Rooney, and an early appearance by the then Cassius Clay, and you've got a hell of a movie.

4: ***Somebody Up There Likes Me*** (1956). Rocky Graziano's life as portrayed by Paul Newman. There's also Steve McQueen and Sal Mineo (are there still Sal Mineo fans out there?). Rent it and see the same grainy look that Martin Scorsese either copped or paid homage to in *Raging Bull*.

5: ***Fat City*** (1972). John Huston directed this forgotten but beautiful baby. Stacy Keach plays another messed-up and washed-out fighter who redis-

covers life by mentoring a young boxing comer. Boxing is a fucked-up sport, a point not missed in this movie.

All right, enough of the back alleys and shady deals of the fight business. Let's get right to an only slightly less karmically corrupt sport. Ladies and germs and idiots alike, I give you the top five football films ever made:

1: *M*A*S*H* (1970). Brilliant film by Robert Altman that features a lengthy football sequence at the end that makes it the funniest gridiron flick ever.

2: **North Dallas Forty** (1979). Football was never more real in the movies than this look at the deep inner lives of players. Nick Nolte is great. Mac Davis is also pretty great. John Matuszak, undeniably dead.

3: **The Longest Yard** (1974). Burt Reynolds did a great job as the quarterback stud stuck in the penitentiary. *HOO-WAH!*

4: **Everybody's All-American** (1988). What becomes a football hero most? See Dennis Quaid and Jessica Lange figure it out.

5: **The Fortune Cookie** (1966). Jack Lemmon plays a cameraman who gets hurt by a football player during a game with hilarious consequences. Lemmon hires a shyster lawyer to bilk the insurance company, providing a goofy plot around some fantastic period shots of real live football games.

OK, on to baseball. Does anyone know why there are so few movies about the game, and why those that exist almost always suck? I don't know either. But check these out:

1: **Bull Durham** (1988). Kevin Costner was so much better in this baseball movie than he was in *Field of Dreams.* Not that I didn't like *Field of Dreams,* but *Bull Durham* is just a lot better. A great movie about life in the minor leagues, especially noteworthy for Susan

Sarandon's from-Mars performance as Durham, North Carolina's leading Baseball Annie.

2: *The Pride of the Yankees* (1942). Gary Cooper as Lou Gehrig, and even better, Babe Ruth as Babe Ruth. See the Bambino talk! See the Sultan of Swat ingest a hot dog! Rent the movie!

3: *Fear Strikes Out* (1957). Tony Perkins plays Jimmy Piersall of my beloved Red Sox in this film about an outfielder going mental. So what's new?

4: *The Bingo Long Traveling All-Stars and Motor Kings* (1976). A tale from the old Negro League days of a barnstorming team that includes James Earl Jones, Billy Dee Williams, and Richard Pryor. Move to the back, Ken Burns, this is the best testament we have on film to the old black ballplayers not allowed to play with the whites.

5: *Field of Dreams* (1989). OK, it gave me chills, I'm a human being, fer chrissakes. Watch it. Bring three hankies. But don't call my radio show and want to talk about it.

Baseball has far more shitty films to call its own than good ones. The two worst, by my learned reckoning, are:

1: *The Babe Ruth Story* (1948). A movie that truly sucks. Starring the terrible William Bendix wearing a ridiculous putty nose, the film portrayed Babe as a goofy village idiot. Bendix couldn't play baseball, couldn't act, and couldn't overcome a script that had the Babe walking into a bar and ordering a glass of milk. But perhaps this terrible movie's most inspirational scene was when Babe merely says "Hiya kid" to a little boy trapped in a wheelchair. Healed by the Babe's words, the kid gets up and walks! *HOO-WAH!* Major suck-ola.

2: *Safe at Home* (1962). Find this gem on the dreck table of your local video store. The movie stars Mickey

Mantle and Roger Maris as two angelic athletes named Mickey Mantle and Roger Maris. The plot tells of a ten-year-old little leaguer who needs to get the two to attend his little league banquet. The athletes, being angels, come. That's the whole movie. In real life, of course, Mickey Mantle was turning New York in 1962 into his own Gomorrah.

Baseball has long blown it when it came to movies, but I was surprised to remember so many good basketball films. The best, I think, are:

1: *White Men Can't Jump* (1992). Wesley Snipes and Woody Harrelson portray two basketball hustlers at war with themselves and the outdoor courts of Los Angeles. Some of the best trash-talking that you'll hear anywhere this side of Larry Bird.

2: *Hoosiers* (1986). You thought Bobby Knight was an asshole to play for? Then check out Gene Hackman as coach of an early-sixties Indiana high school team going for the state championship. The picture has great game action, and Dennis Hopper blows away everybody else in one of the best roles of his wacko career.

3: *The Bachelor and the Bobby-Soxer* (1947). This movie actually stinks, but there's a great basketball sequence at the end that makes it a great goof to watch now. Cary Grant plays a guy who is forced by a judge to take Shirley Temple to a high school basketball game. The game is noteworthy more for its history of a long gone era in basketball when the players were all white and the shorts were unbelievably short.

4: *Fast Break* (1979). Underrated movie that stars Gabe Kaplan as the coach of a small college team from Nevada. Also featuring Bernard King and former UCLA and "Hill Street Blues" star Michael Warren, the movie has good period weirdness. And look for Laurence Fishburne in a teeny-weeny part.

5: *The Absent-minded Professor* (1961). Fred MacMurray plays a professor who invents flying rubber, a.k.a. "flubber." At the end, Fred applies flubber to the shoes of his college's basketball team, allowing white men to finally jump.

Hockey, meantime, has the great *Slap Shot* (1977), about a minor league hockey team who play dirty to survive. Paul Newman is a pisser in this one. And for you roller derby fans, there's always the classic *Kansas City Bomber,* featuring Raquel Welch as the roller mama who pulls other women's hair and punches her way to glory in this unbelievably cheesy movie.

Now strap yourselves in, fellows, we're headed up to the highest reaches of high culture. Everything that's right with humanity can be heard in the opera; everything that's fucked with the world can also be found in the way women are treated in the plots of said extravaganzas. Because I know you all have the approximate attention spans of flies, I will cut to the quick of the stories behind these operas:

1: *Madama Butterfly.* Madam Butterfly is a fifteen-year-old Japanese girl who gets married to an American sailor. Butterfly's family tosses her out of the clan for hitching a white boy, and then the sailor goes home to America, not returning for three years. Butterfly endures, refusing offers from Japanese men in order to wait for the sailor to come back. When he does—with his new American wife—Butterfly kills herself. One more woman taking the gas pipe over a man.

2: *Carmen.* Carmen is a hot gypsy girl working in a cigarette factory who gets involved with Don José, a soldier. Don José, the idiot, goes away for a spell and returns to find that Carmen has taken up with a bullfighter. Pissed, he kills Carmen, the asshole. If Don José were alive today, he would simply hire Johnnie Cochran and get off.

3: *I Pagliacci.* A clown stabs his wife and her lover for betrayal. Buy Pavarotti's version and you'll live in a new realm, you idiots.

4: *Aïda.* Aïda is an Ethiopian slave girl who falls in love with Radames, head of the Egyptian guard. She convinces him to betray the Egyptian army for her love, a crime that gets Radames buried alive with Aïda. That's right, blame the bitch again, you sexist assholes.

And a Final Programming Note from the Fabulous Sports Babe

I'm going on vacation, but I always take care of my fans . . . And especially my stalkers . . . so here's my schedule for the next two weeks:

WEEK 1

Today after the show: Fuel up the Dodge Dart, fill the trunk with Twinkies, lock up the Sportsboy in the "Gimp Box" . . . haul ass out of Petticoat Junction

This weekend: Fly to Dallas, help Michael Irvin clean graffiti off highway overpasses

Monday through Wednesday: Go to South America, torch a couple acres of rain forest

Wednesday night: Stop off in Monterrey, Mexico . . . catch a ballgame and a bacterial infection

Thursday: Go to Times Square . . . pick up some rubber novelty items for the Dennis Rodman wedding

Friday through Sunday: Spend some quality time with my degenerate son, Garth

WEEK 2

Monday: Stop by Whaler offices, drop off a clue . . . and/or pipe bomb

Tuesday: Pick up a a a pack of unfiltered Camels for a card game at Marge Schott's

Wednesday: Just me . . . and my pool noodle

Thursday: Fly all day, make three plane changes to get from Boston to Petticoat Junction

And then: Back in Petticoat Junction for . . . Football Friday!!!

HOO-WAH!!!

Photography Credits